A sound arises out of the earth—

a singing, a friendliness.

—CEDRIC WRIGHT

leaning toward light

light

Poems
for gardens
& the hands
that tend them

EDITED BY
Tess Taylor

FOREWORD BY
Aimee Nezhukumatathil

ILLUSTRATIONS BY
Melissa Castrillón

 Storey Publishing

Contents

Planting & Sprouting

Weeding & Wilding

Growing & Tending

Being & Waiting

Grieving & Release

Harvest & Feeding

Wintering & Turning Again

The Whole World, a Garden

IT SHOULD SURPRISE NO ONE THAT, as a poet, I've been tickled for years to learn that the word *anthology* means a "gathering of flowers." Even if your garden grows vegetables or fruit, flowers need to bloom to make the harvest possible. How perfect, then, to have this gathering, this flowering, of poems about the connection of hand to earth.

The garden is a primer. It teaches us about fellowship with animals, as in Danusha Laméris's poem describing a new relationship with worms: "I want to contribute however I can, / forgetting, a moment, my place on the menu." And a garden teaches us how to take care of each other, as January Gill O'Neil reflects, "What I could not have predicted all those years ago is how much my teenagers would come to love cooking and eating what we grow with our own hands." A garden teaches us how to share and reconnect with others, too. "Have you / noticed the way plants lean, as though longing / for news from a neighbor, a song, a touch, just / a little touch?" asks Jason Myers.

For many poets, the garden also provides a parallel to their art. When writing is going well, time can feel like it is malleable, says my friend Ross Gay, tender of a "janky" garden (his word, not mine). "Gardening," he says, "slows me down. I want to stop and observe everything." A poet's occupation indeed! And the revision—O, the figuring it all out as you go and making mistakes—the garden offers up so much *reward* in revision. As Jennie Xie puts it, "Disorder begins to flare." You can course-correct and have everything to gain, like double the blackberries! Tomatoes through October! "So much / already alive between us, so many blessings / threading our days like the gold of sun, / yet here I stand, holding this bounty, / begging for more," as James Crews admits.

Many contemporary poems treat the garden mainly as a thing over *there*, when in fact, growing is all around us, connecting us, influencing not only our relationship with the outdoors, but our sense of self. The poems gathered here lean toward a more forward-thinking relationship with vegetable, animal, mineral—and each other. As former poetry editor of *Orion* magazine, and current poetry editor of *Sierra*, the storytelling branch of the Sierra Club, I hope to get readers interested in a new, previously unvoiced vision of the possibility and promise of gardens as a haven or refuge.

Further, it's my hope that this bouquet and bounty of poems will appeal to a multicultural generation—one traditionally excluded from most conversations about gardening. For example, through-out most of my schooling, I was never taught any gardening poems from writers of color. And the stakes are different for our world these days. I'm so grateful more of us recognize the fact that gardening is not and has never been a tending of the earth by just one group of people. It's high time anthologies—these bouquets—acknowledge this. As Ashley M. Jones says in "Photosynthesis," "This is the work we have always known— / pulling food and flowers from a pile of earth. / The difference, now: my father is not a slave, / not a sharecropper."

When I first started writing poems, I was also rarely, if ever, exposed to any gardening poems by Asian American women— poems that might have included motherhood and sensuality *and* brown skin *and* the outdoors, so I think a tiny part of me thought it was forbidden in some way. When you see an absence and void of your body and your hopes and desires in American letters, what does that do to a young writer? How could that not motivate me to write my way into a garden that until very recently ignored people who look (and love) like me?

It's thrilling, then, to see in these pages a reflection of the world I want to live in. One that interdepends on people who love and look and move through this world differently than I do. As a mother to two boys, it's imperative for me to share books and journals and poems with them that showcase this variety, this vibrancy, so that they grow up not only seeing themselves reflected in the books they read but also feeling a sense of possibility and potential in their own imaginations and future gardens.

I'm constantly searching for ways to connect and nurture future generations with a deep appreciation and awe of nature that carries with it a robust sense of place and belonging. Rachel Carson's wish for every child to have "a sense of wonder so indestructible that it would last throughout life" seems needed now more than ever to encourage a new sense of gentleness toward what we can grow in a pot on our windowsill, on our decks, or in a backyard plot of soil. And maybe that goodwill will then be extended toward other people on our planet, and toward our neighbors.

*"If you look the right way, you can see that
the whole world is a garden."*
—Frances Hodgson Burnett, *The Secret Garden*

Perhaps there's an even simpler reason for why we need this anthology of garden poems: The mysteries of wonder and the desire to make things grow and germinate urge us to seek explanations in the innocent belief that whatever we come to understand—about tending, about the soil that feeds us—cannot ever truly be lost.

Hopefully the book you have in hand, what you might clutch to your heart, what you might highlight on a screen or perhaps dog-ear with a thumb, can remind you for many years to harvest your own simple bounty, one that you can't buy with a click of your mouse. We all need to put our hands (and shovels and rakes!) into the soil, a dark universe of infinite possibilities if we have but some sun, some water, some care.

Gardening in Public

URING THE WORST MONTHS OF THE COVID-19 pandemic, when I'd suffered several losses and felt raw and isolated, I spent a great deal of time in our garden. At our bungalow, where the light in the front is best, this meant spending hours in our postage-stamp-size yard. I renewed beds, fertilized fruit trees, and reclaimed the sunny, unused concrete driveway for planters of favas, pole beans, and tomatillos. The labor steadied me, and had an additional benefit: As I worked, I often fell into conversation with passersby. I was grateful to be growing both kale and community—in a difficult time, I tended the garden and the garden also tended back.

It isn't the first time a garden has renewed me. As a teenager who struggled with disordered eating, seasons spent planting, sowing, and harvesting helped me understand how both the earth and I deserve and need wise and gentle care. After that, I found a way to garden pretty much everywhere I went: I led a teen garden program at a youth center in Berkeley, built a community garden in a formerly vacant lot in Brooklyn, and worked on a small farm in the Berkshires. Each season rewarded me with birdsong, soilcraft, and friendship. I saw how gardens help us nourish both the soil and one another.

Gardeners, are, by their nature, people who believe in regeneration, as poet Laura Villareal points out. They understand that the broken world we inherit can also be amended, with compost, worms, and steady tending. They have seen that the tended earth, in turn, offers up radical abundance—not only of food, but of insects, birds, rhizomes, and soil. The garden surprises us in unexpected

*Sometimes, in the face of huge pain,
the things of the earth can help reroute any of us
toward awe and fascination.*

ways. Oregano winters over. Wild miner's lettuce springs back.
A volunteer pumpkin luxuriates near the compost bin. Suddenly
met with abundance, we beg people to come help harvest our
plums. We befriend a plot of earth, and it befriends us in return.
By some powerful force, this friendship brings us into a fuller,
more just communion with the human and nonhuman at once.

Of course, any garden plot is small compared to the brokenness
of a wider world that can seem beyond mending. We live in
a divided society. We live inside climate change, ecosystem loss,
mass extinction, and racial violence, in a global community gripped
by famine, hunger, and war. The heaviest days are excruciating.
Yet sometimes, in the face of huge pain, the things of the earth—
hummingbird and mockingbird, snail and earthworm—can help
reroute any of us toward awe and fascination. They can reconnect us—
if just for a moment—with the life-energy we need to go on.
Gardens also remind us that repair need not be so far off: In daily
ways, we can each build our lives toward greater diversity and
abundance. Nobody needs to be hungry. When we work the right
way, we can all be fed.

My life outside being a gardener is being a poet. When I was
asked to craft an anthology of new gardening poems, my heart
leapt in delight. Poems and gardens share congruence: Gardens
distill nature, helping us see how to live inside what we must wisely
steward. Poems distill language, creating sculptural spaces that
illuminate the world around us, allowing us to savor the language
through which any one thing can be known. Poems and gardens

sculpt what the poet John Keats called "slow time"—building up sites from which we may apprehend and savor our wider life. Poems and gardens also remind us, in the words of poet Gwendolyn Brooks, that

> we are each other's
> harvest:
> we are each other's
> business:
> we are each other's
> magnitude and bond.

In gardens and poems we find figures for grief and surprise, for loss and regeneration. Gardens and poems each help us dwell and abide.

The garden poem is as ancient as literature itself. After all, acts of hand, song, labor, and voice are deeply welded. Yet as I weeded through a great stack of gardening anthologies, I realized that many felt quite historic. Others were academic, tracing the history of garden literature from the important insight that the English word *paradise* comes from a Persian word for "walled garden." I came to this project with a new question in mind: What does it mean to garden in the early twenty-first century, in a deracinated, accelerating world, when the natural world is collapsing, and where, despite enormous technological advances, we have not yet managed to cultivate widespread abundance, nourishment, or peace?

This anthology collects poets who address these questions. It celebrates current acts of digging and feeding, while acknowledging this moment's particular brokenness. Like a year, it moves through planting and toward harvest. Like a garden, it offers space for grief and reverie. I am American, and, with some exceptions, these poets are, too. From this moment and vantage, they sing about tending and attentiveness, reminding us of our connections to food, pleasure, soil, and one another. Some poets, like Mariana Goycoechea, find strength in watering just one houseplant. Others, like Danusha Laméris, grieve the loss of a child. Others, like Keetje Kuipers and Ellen Bass, celebrate the sensual shape of a garden. In aggregate, this collection reminds us that poems and gardens reward the efforts of attention: The tending we do inside them repays us.

In a difficult time, these poems also garden in public. Like my front-yard artichokes, they help us strike up conversation, reminding us as Ashley M. Jones does, that "it is a conversational labor, gardening." Sometimes the conversation is with other humans, and sometimes it is with soil or animals or bees or our very time on Earth itself. We talk, as Brenda Hillman does, with plants. And these conversations, across realms, sustain us. Like the hyphae that hold a healthy soil together, these poems tendril out, acting as connectors.

Over the pandemic months, I noticed that I was not the only one putting stakes down in the front yard. Up and down streets in my small town, gardens sprung up in front and side yards, in planters and on lawns. We have reinvested in community gardens.

We build the good ecosystem together; in it,
we are each nourished and fed.

Even now I am gathering donations for a community orchard I'd like to help steward. Earlier this season, a neighbor stopped by with fog-resistant tomato starts. Even now I am watching Ari, my neighbor across the street, hitch up a found stake for the young fig tree she is planting in her formerly dusty lot. Her front and side yards are currently full of herbs; blackberries; a pea trellis made of an old laundry rack. Her yard, where people now often come to chat and swap plants, is a generous reminder that under the skin of the barren, there is always the possibility of greater abundance.

I honor the abundance in these poems—the way they dig beneath ordinary life and sprout to remind us of life's power and shimmer. They also remind us that we build the good ecosystem together; that in it, we are each nourished and fed. I keep thinking of the words of Cornel West: "Justice is what love looks like in public." Gardens are what hope looks like in public. And these poems are also emblems of that hope.

—TESS TAYLOR

ROSS GAY

A Small Needful Fact

Is that Eric Garner worked
for some time for the Parks and Rec.
Horticultural Department, which means,
perhaps, that with his very large hands,
perhaps, in all likelihood,
he put gently into the earth
some plants which, most likely,
some of them, in all likelihood,
continue to grow, continue
to do what such plants do, like house
and feed small and necessary creatures,
like being pleasant to touch and smell,
like converting sunlight
into food, like making it easier
for us to breathe.

Planting & Sprouting

Be humble as soil and you will see
every particle of soil is drunk on Love—

—RUMI

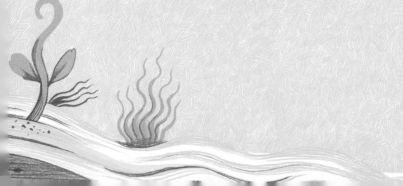

ASHLEY M. JONES

BECOMING NEW & NEW BECOMING

When I think of spring, I think of the world becoming new. I think of the rain making things grow. I think of my dad in the backyard garden, getting the ground ready to receive all the flowers and vegetables and fruits. During the first part of the pandemic, we all hunkered down at my parents' house and had a beautiful summer harvest. Dad spent weekends in the garden. I spent my days and nights on Zoom, but there was always a beautiful part of the morning or late afternoon when Dad would bring the harvest in. Sometimes it was a handful of carrots. Maybe some lemons off his beloved little tree. Maybe some tomatoes for sandwiches or a salad. Maybe a bouquet of herbs. Whatever he brought, it was good and it tasted like his love. Like the security you have when you know your family wants you and you want it. That sustenance. That spring.

Glazed Carrots

4	bunches tender baby carrots, the sweeter the better
2–3	tablespoons butter
¼	cup honey
2	teaspoons cinnamon
	Dash of cumin and red pepper flakes (optional)
	Pinch of salt
	Parsley and lemon, for garnish

Preheat oven to 400°F (200°C). Peel and trim all carrots, but leave them mostly whole. Lightly layer them, not more than two carrots deep, in a roasting pan. Add butter, honey, spices, and salt. Roast for 35 minutes or until tender. Garnish with chopped parsley and lemon.

WENDELL BERRY

FROM *Prayers and Sayings of the Mad Farmer*

Sowing the seed,
my hand is one with the earth.

Wanting the seed to grow,
my mind is one with the light.

Hoeing the crop,
my hands are one with the rain.

Having cared for the plants,
my mind is one with the air.

Hungry and trusting,
my mind is one with the earth.

Eating the fruit,
my body is one with the earth.

ASHLEY M. JONES

Photosynthesis

When I was young, my father taught us
how dirt made way for food,
how to turn over soil so it would hold a seed,
an infant bud, how the dark could nurse it
until it broke its green arms out to touch the sun.
In every backyard we've ever had, he made a little garden plot
with room for heirloom tomatoes, corn, carrots,
peppers: jalapeno, bell, and poblano—
okra, eggplant, lemons, collards, broccoli, pole beans,
watermelon, squash, trees filled with fruit and nuts,
brussels sprouts, herbs: basil, mint, parsley, rosemary—
onions, sweet potatoes, cucumber, cantaloupe, cabbage,
oranges, swiss chard and peaches,
sunflowers tall and straightbacked as soldiers,
lantana, amaryllis, echinacea,
pansies and roses and bushes bubbling with hydrangeas.
Every plant with its purpose—
flowers to bring worms and wasps. Even their work matters here.

This is the work we have always known—
pulling food and flowers from a pile of earth.
The difference, now: my father is not a slave,
not a sharecropper. This land is his and so is this garden,
so is this work. The difference is that he owns this labor.
The work of his own hands for his own belly,
for his own children's bellies. We eat because he works.

This is the legacy of his grandmother, my great-granny—
Ollie Mae Harris and her untouchable flower garden.
Just like her hats, her flowerbeds sprouted something special,
plants and colors the neighbors could only dream of.
He was young when he learned that this beauty is built on work—
the cows and the factories in their stomachs,
the fertilizer they spewed out—
the stink that brought such fragrance. What you call waste,
I call power. What you call work I make beautiful again.

In his garden, even problems become energy, beauty—
my father has ended many work days in the backyard,
worries of the firehouse dropping like grain, my father wrist-deep
in soil. I am convinced the earth speaks back to him
as he feeds it—it is a conversational labor, gardening.
The seeds tell him what they will be, the soil tells seeds how to grow,
my father speaks sun and water into the earth,
we hear him, each harvest, his heartbeat sweet, like fruit.

Greenbriar Lane

How long are we going to have this problem with rent?
Someone asks. I'm on the back patio planting begonias
in coffee-black earth. My job is to bring beautiful
things back to life. When I hear, through the windows,
men call my name, I turn—they're not there.

COLE SWENSEN

Gardening

—as opposed to a garden—is always seen in extreme close-up. The hand that pinches back an errant sprout, or the hand that picks up a tool and thinks that the hand is as much a part of the garden as any of its other fruits.

Three Sunflower Seeds

before I push
the dark seeds into the dirt,
preparing the dirt

•

waiting
for a beginning—
roomfuls of gold

•

patience
I say to the empty vase
my heart

AIMEE NEZHUKUMATATHIL

Spring (a conversation)

—from Lace & Pyrite, *with Ross Gay*

No shadows here, only mud.
Praise the caked-up trowel, hand rake,
and grass scissor. I want to kiss each crumble
of sunbaked earth as my sons welcome iris
and drunk ants whirl-rush over each juicy peony bud.
After warm rains come the spring peepers shivering
out of the mud and sitting half in, half out of a puddle.
You must know the bees have come early
this year too: I see them visit aster, sweet Williams,
bleeding hearts, and azalea blossoms hardy enough
to not have crisped with the last late frost. Whatever light
bees give off after the last snow, I hold up to you now.
I cannot explain the click-step of beetles.
You are on your own for that. I grew up with patience
for soil and stars. Lace and pyrite. I believe
in an underworld littered with gems.
In another life, I have to. Sometimes I lose track
of all the bees and their singing.
You thought I said *stinging*.

LAUREN MOSELEY

Planting Inkberry Hollies During the Pandemic

Not blackberries but
Black berries

Were what we wanted
The woman at the nursery

Said we needed
One male plant and one female

How far apart should we plant them?
At least six feet

And how close?
Within twenty but not around a corner

They need to see each other
To talk to each other

Trapeze

Sky-bound in someone's yard,
bluebells poke out of dirt.

From back-alley I swing
open our gate to garden.

Beneath the skin your fist
punches: harbinger bud.

A shoot sprouts after snow—
you practice somersaults—

and autumn bulbs now show:
hyacinth, snowdrop, crocus.

How much space will you need
to grow? A galaxy

of cells, then the heartbeat.
You nose-dive down. A dove

hoo, hoo, hooing. Above
lodestar, a slip of moon.

LAURA VILLAREAL

What Regenerates in a Household

The base of a store-bought celery can grow more celery
with enough water. In the plush light of our apartment window,

growth comes when no one is watching.
It sprouts stalk & lace leaves while we are at your brother's wedding

in a place where palm trees aren't native but symbolic.
Like you, I fumble in our kitchen drawers for the easy metaphor.

Liken a regenerating plant to myself. Cut
cheese for crackers before dinner. You are hungry

wanting to know how to write about daily life.
I tell you writing about sadness is easy. Joy comes

in explosions. I learn something new every day
to break the line between repetition. It's so easy

finding wonder in the dust lining of baseboards
when I zoom in. I find a single hair, long and mine.

You call them recuerdos when I apologize,
ways to find me in our home when I'm not around.

What regenerates in a household is not as miraculous as celery,
it doesn't grow unwatched either. But feels like a miracle anyways.

CLEOPATRA MATHIS

Earth

You see a woman of a certain age,
not old, yet seeing every sign
of how the world will change her.
More and more, you'll find her in the garden
but not for onions or potatoes.
She wants blooms, color,
a breaking in the earth's disorder.
Swollen branch, the right bird—
they can make her cry. And the fussing
over moving this or that to the right location.
Learning to be alone,
she brings out ten varieties of rose,
armed against pest or blight
and the cutting northern cold
she fights with blankets of dirt.
Earliest spring will find her hovering
over the waxy perfection of tulips, the ones
closest to the thawing ground.
You'd think it's the opening she loves,
the loosening flower revealing
the meticulous still-life deep in the cup.
But what she needs is to see
those stiff-petaled, utterly still ones
rise out of the dirt.

The weather won't cooperate. She sinks
hundreds of bulbs in the rain,
mud on her hands, black smear on her neck.
For this birthing, all she pays
is stiff joints, and she knows again
the insistence of flowering.
Falling, she knows the flowers
fall to the season, and the seasons
to the great wheel. Fallen, she's learned
to prefer the fallen.

ANDY EATON

Autumn Blooming Cherry

Still staff-like and slender, risen
from its plastic pot, the new
branches appear each week
and bear these tooth-edged

greens. Late spring, out here
watching if watch is what to say
I do, so slow a tree's emergence
on our deck. Sapling,

two shades of leaves breaking
across what will come to be
its higher, pink-white bloom
and crown. Late, I sit back

and let what star might rise
from out my mouth dissolve.
Someday we will live somewhere
we can put this in the ground.

Foreday in the Morning

My mother grew morning glories that spilled onto the walkway
    toward her porch
Because she was a woman with land who showed as much by giving
    it color.
She told me I could have whatever I worked for. That means she
    was an American.
But she'd say it was because she believed
In God. I am ashamed of America
And confounded by God. I thank God for my citizenship in spite
Of the timer set on my life to write
These words: I love my mother. I love black women
Who plant flowers as sheepish as their sons. By the time the blooms
Unfurl themselves for a few hours of light, the women who tend them
Are already at work. Blue. I'll never know who started the lie that
    we are lazy,
But I'd love to wake that bastard up
At foreday in the morning, toss him in a truck, and drive him under God
Past every bus stop in America to see all those black folk
Waiting to go work for whatever they want. A house? A boy
To keep the lawn cut? Some color in the yard? My God, we leave
    things green.

Weeding & Wilding

What would the world be, once bereft
Of wet and wildness? Let them be left,
O let them be left, wildness and wet;
Long live the weeds, and the wilderness yet.

—GERARD MANLEY HOPKINS

JANE HIRSHFIELD

IN PRAISE OF STRONG SEEDLINGS

For many years, I didn't grow fava beans in my garden because the large plants take room but yield very little if you end up using only the twice-shelled inner bean. Favas are delicious, elegant, jewel-vivid in their bright green color, one of the essence-of-spring foodstuffs ... but tiny. Then one year, after particularly early and heavy fall rains, I decided to try again when I found paper packets of favas in a community farm's seed-lending library in Richmond, California. The plants did splendidly—the strong seedlings evaded the pulling beaks of birds, and eventually the stems were covered in big black-and-white flowers, then in beans that ripened, a half-dozen or so at a time, into enormous pods. I did an online search and found that of course you can use the pods whole. The recipe I adapted is intended for a cooled plate of Turkish meze, but I eat the beans warm, over quinoa, brown rice, or whole-wheat couscous, with some bright salad on the side.

Braised Fava Beans

This braising method would work for any broad bean, though I prefer my summer-season whole-pod beans a bit more crisp; sometimes I eat them while still standing out with the plants. (I've grown Dragon's Tongue beans now for decades—the first were a gift from poet Sandra Alcosser's Montana garden.) Favas, though, want to be thoroughly softened, and eating them in March, as I am now, the weather is still cool enough that this warming braise preparation feels seasonally right.

3 tablespoons olive oil
½ yellow onion, coarsely diced
   Lemon zest
   Herbs of choice
1 pound fava beans, ends trimmed and cut in thirds
1 cup water or vegetable broth

   Salt and pepper
1 teaspoon sugar (optional)
   Soy sauce or liquid aminos (optional)
1 tablespoon flour
   More herbs and/or yogurt topping (optional)

Heat the olive oil in a skillet. Add the yellow onion and cook until transparent. Add a little lemon zest or any other herb or seasoning in the direction of your choice—a few branches of tarragon or thyme, some dill, cumin, coriander, Chinese five-spice, smoked paprika, chipotle chile.

Add the fava bean pods. (My beans have no tough string needing removal, whether because of the unknown variety or because they've been picked minutes before being used.) Sauté the pods briefly, then add a cup of water or vege-table broth, some salt and pepper, an optional teaspoon of sugar, an optional bit of soy sauce or liquid aminos, and a tablespoon of flour. Mix well. Turn the heat to low and cover with a loose lid; cook for 15 to 20 minutes, making sure the liquid doesn't all boil off.

Remove the lid and continue to simmer until the sauce reaches the desired thickness. Test for salt, and season further in whatever direction suits. Fresh chopped parsley works well as does lemon juice (you can use the lemon you zested). In the Turkish recipe, you'd allow the beans to cool and then serve with yogurt infused with minced garlic and topped with dill.

Weed

Its precondition
is uselessness—
wrong in its place,
bobbing in wind,
fattening in sun, red
seeds in a cloak
with an orange ruff
whatever that is,
Bittersweet, maybe.

JACK JOHNSON

Stained Glass
(for Hart)

Deep in the compost, down
to when my son was seven,
the blade of my shovel
splits the rotted body
of a vacuum bag–limp
swirls of hair, bread tab, paper
clip, red Lego block,
gray sword and helmet, blue
head and body of the Square Knight.

I rake the garden.
His yellow battle-ax appears.
A prickly green clump turns into a tree.

A rotted onion-half
turns into a horse,
sprouting green legs, upside
down in the black soil.

These pieces like stained glass—
my son in a shaft of living room light
assails a castle.

Deep Lane

When I'm down on my knees pulling up wild mustard
by the roots before it sets seed, hauling the old ferns
further into the shade, I'm talking to the anvil of darkness:

break-table, slab no blow could dent
rung with the making, and out of that chop and rot
comes the fresh surf of the lupines.

When the shovel slips into white root-flesh,
into the meat coursing with cool water,
when I'm grubbing on my knees, what is the hammer?

Dusky skin of the tuber, naked worms
who write on the soil every letter,
my companion blind, all day we go digging,

harrowing, rooting deep. Spade-plunge
and trowel, sweet turned-down gas flame
slow-charring carbon, out of which sprouts

the wild unsayable.
Beauty's the least of it:
you get ready,

like Deborah, who used to garden in the dark,
hauling out candles and a tall glass of what she said was tea,
and digging and reading and studying in the dirt.

She'd bring a dictionary. If study is prayer, she said, I'm praying.
If you've already gone down to the anvil, if you've rested your face
on that adamant, maybe you're already changed.

FROM Tending

A walk through the garden sets off the mind's tripwires.

This year, the wisteria murmur. Then ring, out of season.

The light: raucous
or the light: slow and scummed.

Which is it?

One hour loosens
from the socket of another.

The rain's not yet done, but the light comes feeling

its way back, as it does.
The interior smells fecund.

But this greening's abbreviated by the carbon-blade of shears.

One self prunes violently at all the others
thinking she's the gardener.

Even so, the blossoms drip.
Spill over.
A few inches above, the sticky murmur of flies.

Disorder begins to flare.

There are roots long in the earth, and they hasten.

And pink worms, out of sight,
with their dim impulse to let the dirt churn through them.

DANA LEVIN

Golden Poppy

Going outside to weed and catching a poppy opening—
    the little paper cap enclosing it

    starting to split—

You really could see it—bud unfurling—if you were
    still enough, if you were close—

How uneasy I'd been, in my dream, eyes closed
    and someone's fingers moving over them—

moving over them, someone said, because the feeler
    was blind—and she needed to try on my skin.

My eyes snapped open—to find myself
    the blind feeler, eyes milked over—a guiding

woman at each arm—so open and curious
    as she learned by feeling—the contours

of my face—the blind-me the better me, the skin-me
    reluctant, wary—

48

I bent closer: poppy curled tight inside a paper cap,
    golden spiral, pushing out—

    We would have to open

the way everything opened—by splitting apart
    what held us in—

THOM GUNN

Considering the Snail

The snail pushes through a green
night, for the grass is heavy
with water and meets over
the bright path he makes, where rain
has darkened the earth's dark. He
moves in a wood of desire,

pale antlers barely stirring
as he hunts. I cannot tell
what power is at work, drenched there
with purpose, knowing nothing.
What is a snail's fury? All
I think is that if later

I parted the blades above
the tunnel and saw the thin
trail of broken white across
litter, I would never have
imagined the slow passion
to that deliberate progress.

DANUSHA LAMÉRIS

Feeding the Worms

Ever since I found out that earth worms have taste buds
all over the delicate pink strings of their bodies,
I pause dropping apple peels into the compost bin, imagine
the dark, writhing ecstasy, the sweetness of apples
permeating their pores. I offer beets and parsley,
avocado and melon, the feathery tops of carrots.

I'd always thought theirs a menial life, eyeless and hidden,
almost vulgar—though now, it seems, they bear a pleasure
so sublime, so decadent, I want to contribute however I can,
forgetting, a moment, my place on the menu.

VICTORIA CHANG

Spring Planting

Today I plant bougainvillea and hyacinth. Tomorrow, crocus
and candied pansies.

I am gardening, but my mind is tilling. The crows enter my yard.
They remind me of ink slabs

Chinese calligraphers used—not until mixed with water did
their black ink breathe and broth.

Each morning, goat hairbrush in hand, they sat near willows,
against a dropping moon, drew

all they knew of mist, of hillocks, of lightning behind mulberries.
How strange to think that in just one stroke,

they left themselves on the page. Today, you call to say
you've found a new woman,

not a pretty one, but one like a kind of high-quality porcelain
that stands up to daily use.

You say the word *ring*. I drop my spade. Was it *rain* or *wing*?
No, I am wrong.

And the crow I hate descends on the gate, as if to say *poor fool*.
You tell me she is a heart surgeon.

I imagine her suturing thread into others, recording onto paper
the opening and closing of the heart.

The crow cries in couplets. I bend to pull out another row
of palsied phlox you had planted last spring.

JANE HIRSHFIELD

The Contract

The woman who gave me the rosebush
reminds me:
"Cut it back hard."

The stems resist.

Thorns and weedy twig-thickets
catch on jacket sleeve, on gloves.
Core-wood splinters green under the shears.

Impossible to believe
that so little left will lead to fragrance.

Still, my hands move quickly,
adding their signature branch by branch,
agreeing to loss.

TESS TAYLOR

Now the Artichokes

cluster, prickling with secret.
Each hides sweetness
under a mace

of lapped dragon scales.
What hunger drove shepherds
to eat the first thistle?

The tall ones, past harvest,
explode into blossom:
Violet anemones, cyclops eyes.

What we cannot eat
now dazzles the bees:
I too would romp

in that wild
phosphorescence,
would nectar & stumble

& plunder each bract—

Thistle

under the freeway
      among orange peels
      & diaper boxes hurled
      from windows
      of passing cars

a thistle persists
      jagged leaves brandish
      tiny knives

they glitter under moonlight
animals keep away

violet prickles
      defy drought

thick white roots
      burrow deep below
      concrete

reach out past
      oleander
       & tumbleweeds

a thistle
bends toward light
      despite the all

Fennel

High fog, white sky
Above me on the bouldered hill
Where I
Stumble between head-high
And scattered clumps of weed
—Fennel, of which I once thought seed
Made you invisible.
Each forms a light green mist
—Feathery auras, though the look deceives,
For looked at closely they consist
Of tiny leading into tinier leaves
In which each fork is sharply separate.
Yet tender, touched: I pinch a sprig and sniff,
And it reminds me of
The other times I have pinched fennel sprigs
For this fierce poignancy.
I stand here as if lost,
As if invisible on this broken cliff,
Invisible sky above.
And for a second I float free
Of personality, and die
Into my senses, into the unglossed
Unglossable
Sweet and transporting yet attaching smell
—The very agent that releases me
Holding me here, as well.

Dear Damselfly

All summer long, the red-fur rhubarb crosses over.

Spirits fight up through the scallions
wasps shadow the crocuses
with their family talk.

I travel from June to June
seeking a beauty like yours:
kiss-shaped, unstandardized
coptering the long grass
like a news flight over Manhattan.

What have I loved? The tended soil
and the thrashing that breaks it.

Gray-skinned stems, dying and alive
cycle up the lattice. Bees drone the sound-wound
the sunny hum of community.

You with your smoke-eyes are all-seeing
predaceous and singular over lake waters.

De-root me from this garden.

Growing & Tending

Pulling weeds, picking stones,
we are made of dreams and bones
—DAVID MALLET

ANN FISHER-WIRTH

TENDRILS OF LIFE
& COMMUNITY

A harvest is about food, but also about people. It evokes a time
and place.

Fresh tomato pie, which I used to make when our kids were
still at home, conjures up our early years in Oxford, Mississippi,
where we've lived since 1988. In our early years here, our wonder-
ful independent bookstore, Square Books, had an upstairs café
run by Mary Hartwell Howorth, champion gardener and sister-
in-law of the bookstore owner, Richard Howorth. Every once in a
while, one of her café recipes would show up in the monthly peri-
odical advertising new books—et voilà, the recipe for tomato pie.
The pie's spicy dressing also makes me remember another chef,
Angelo Mistilis, who has since passed away. He had run a restau-
rant on College Hill, but we knew him as a neighbor who passed
the day on his front porch swing, always ready to call a greeting.
He was a local legend, not only for his hamburger steaks and
fries, but also for his unfailing friendliness and kindness. One
story I love is that he used to provide art supplies for the men
around the corner at the old city jail, and buy and display what
they made.

Tomatoes are the quintessential summer harvest. For years
I grew them in the raised-bed garden my son built in our side
yard—a small garden but, at first, wildly fertile. The high point was
one steaming July day when just four plants yielded 13 pounds of
tomatoes, my pea vines snaked graceful and fat with pods toward
the sky, and one of my zucchinis grew so huge that in desperation
I tried to use it for gazpacho. Now I grow flowers, not vegetables;

that same raised bed is full of daffodils and irises, a gardenia bush, white and scarlet roses.

Thinking of tomatoes evokes those years in the '80s and '90s, when we were first learning to make Oxford, Mississippi, our new home. It evokes Square Books, a phenomenal cultural center all these years, and the Square Books café with its yummy egg and olive sandwiches, tomato pie, and mint-chocolate frosted brownies. And it evokes memories of Angelo and his wife, JoDale, chatting as we passed by—two neighbors who always made us feel welcome. Of such memories the tendrils of a life, a community, are made.

Feta, Tomato & Basil Pie

1 partially baked pie shell
4 medium tomatoes, peeled, sliced, and drained
1 cup Parmesan cheese
1 cup Angelo's Feta Cheese Dressing
  Garlic and basil, to taste
1 tablespoon cornstarch
  Cracker crumbs

ANGELO'S FETA CHEESE DRESSING

¼ pound feta cheese, crumbled (1 cup)
1½ cups vegetable oil
½ cup white vinegar
¼ cup grated white onion
2 tablespoons capers, drained and chopped
2 garlic cloves, minced
1 teaspoon ground white pepper
½ teaspoon dried oregano
½ teaspoon salt

Fill pie shell with tomatoes. Combine Parmesan, feta cheese dressing, garlic, basil, and cornstarch; spread over tomatoes. Sprinkle cracker crumbs on top. Bake at 350°F (180°C) for 20 minutes.

Trying

I'd forgotten how much
I like to grow things, I shout
to him as he passes me to paint
the basement. I'm trellising
the tomatoes in what's called
a Florida weave. Later, we try
to knock me up again. We do it
in the guest room because that's
the extent of our adventurism
in a week of violence in Florida
and France. Afterward,
the sun still strong though lowering
inevitable to the horizon, I check
on the plants in the back, my
fingers smelling of sex and tomato
vines. Even now, I don't know much
about happiness. I still worry
and want an endless stream of more,
but some days I can see the point
in growing something, even if
it's just to say I cared enough.

JANICE LEE

FROM *Separation Anxiety*

the tomato plants teach
me how to deal
with each kind of person

the puffed-up pigeon repeatedly chases off his foes
not for extra crumbs but to prove that he *can*

the pigeons
show us potential hierarchies
in the making
shifting only when we put our phones down
to encounter the pigeon
on the same ground

trust me

getting down on your knees
would do you some good
hold the intention in your belly
then,
look around
rather than
ahead

Haecceitas

—After Christopher Smart

For the tomato is an orb of holy light.

For its seeds are the defenders of heaven.

For if the vine grow freely it will scale the vault of the stars.

MARIANA GOYCOECHEA

Palm Sunday

Out the window I see
the abuelitas in purple
& the conveniently devout
rushing & showing off their
knotted fronds

like the ones dying
in my bathroom. Mami
taught me to name plants
after those who gifted them.
So I buy plants in this lonely
world
       & name them after myself.

Mariana is dying in the bathroom.

She's a chore to water.
A castaway island of a plant.
I remind her that she, like her mother,
is a child of catastrophe & chaos
as I finally rest her in a tray of water.

I hear Mami saying, *Bueno,*
it's not the first time you
kill yourself.
La luna renews itself
       & so can you.

ALAN CHAZARO

Photosynthesis: (Chinaka Hodge Hosts a Block Party)

Everything begins by absorbing hydrogen   from dirt as DJs
          spin 90s r&b   with weedsmoke, and wet skin

becomes the oxygen of our bodydance—and it begins
               with inhalation: roots; rhubarb;
               sunflowers; the hot

                         stench of chicken mess;
                              a thick aerosol

of summer paints; fat

Adidas laces and barbershop fades; the mixing
of light with dark and dark
          with liquor. I'll say the names

          of these neighborhood trees out loud:

Southern Magnolia, Maidenhair, Chinese Flame, Kentucky Coffee

          and I'll ask what our cosmology is

if not this—and when I say cosmology know

                              I mean blessings,
                         and when I say

blessing, I mean this Sunday afternoon, because darkness is a prayer
　　　　　that must come

over us, it is the promise of empty parking lots
filled with movements that can be traced
back to foot-stepped rhythms and chain-link fences, the neon
blaze of a nosering on a woman's brown nose—

and it begins
　　　　　by observing the astronomy of our limbs while

　　remembering to sip whatever slow-
honey is poured from your lips

　　like the garden in my throat

as your voice
　　　　　becomes this shovel　　　　　becomes my hands

　　　　　digging your waist—

CLAUDIA MONPERE

Mara Mara, Garden Child

You're learning to let the babies grow on the vine.
Still you set your pacifier down

        pluck a tiny cucumber
        cradling it in your palms   murmuring baby, baby, baby

        searching for larger cucumbers
        to make a family.

        We make leaf
        soup with the fallen: apricot leaves, fig, pear, apple.

Yellow song. Amber speech.
I ponder the conversation

        of roots   make twig art   wonder why this bee
        gathers nectar and pollen so methodically
        from each salvia bloom

        while that one is all
                kinetic energy
                       and helium atoms.

I don't wonder about tomorrows
in heat-cracked soil.

It's now.   I want every child
    to fill gaps with carrots   to shape a shrine of soil

and sky, to sail
    sadness far, far away   on their

                yellow leaf boats.

C. D. WRIGHT

Song of the Gourd

In gardening I continued to sit on my side of the car: to
drive whenever possible at the usual level of distraction:
in gardening I shat nails glass contaminated dirt and
threw up on the new shoots: in gardening I learned to
praise things I had dreaded: I pushed the hair out of my
face: I felt less responsible for one man's death one
woman's long-term isolation: my bones softened: in
gardening I lost nickels and ring settings I uncovered
buttons and marbles: I lay half the worm aside and
sought the rest: I sought myself in the bucket and won-
dered why I came into being in the first place: in gar-
dening I turned away from the television and went
around smelling of offal and inedible parts of the
chicken: in gardening I said excelsior: in gardening I re-
quired no company I had to forgive my own failure to
perceive how things were: I went out barelegged at
dusk and dug and dug and dug: I hit rock my ovaries
softened: in gardening I was protean as in no other
realm before or since: I longed to torch my old belong-
ings and belch a little flame of satisfaction: in gardening
I longed to stroll farther into soundlessness: I could al-
most forget what happened many swift years ago in
Arkansas: I felt like a god from down under: chthonian:
in gardening I thought this is it body and soul I am
home at last: excelsior: praise the grass: in gardening I

fled the fold that supported the war: only in gardening
could I stop shrieking: stop: stop the slaughter: only in
gardening could I press my ear to the ground to hear
my soul let out an unyielding noise: my lines softened: I
turned the water onto the joy-filled boychild: only in
gardening did I feel fit to partake to go on trembling in
the last light: I confess the abject urge to weed your
beds while the bittersweet overwhelmed my daylilies: I
summoned the courage to grin: I climbed the hill with
my bucket and slept like a dipper in the cool of your
body: besotted with growth; shot through by green

Gift

A day so happy.
Fog lifted early, I worked in the garden.
Hummingbirds were stopping over honeysuckle flowers.
There was no thing on earth I wanted to possess.
I knew no one worth my envying him.
Whatever evil I had suffered, I forgot.
To think that once I was the same man did not embarrass me.
In my body I felt no pain.
When straightening up, I saw the blue sea and sails.

BRIAN SIMONEAU

Poem Beginning with a Line from Wordsworth

It is a beauteous evening, calm and free,
and the neighbor has shoveled his horseshit
in the garden, bucket after bucket
dumped from rusting pickup to veggie beds,

tomato plants staked with splintered handles
of rakes, cucumbers vined through chicken wire
strung from nail-studded two-by-fours braced
by scrap leather, by snapped fan belts, even

the cinder-blocked Charger sprouting lilac
through its shattered windshield, oil drums halved
for onions and carrots, coffee cans hung
to gather rain in apple-heavy limbs

above the swing where he sits with his wife
when evenings are beauteous, calm and free.

CYNTHIA ROTH

In the Dark

When I am awake alone at night
I water the fern hanging on the porch.

I smoke to see how the wind
can move in one direction

then swirl into invisible silent funnels
above my head or at my feet.

Smoke and street light, crickets, frogs,
the couple next door making love.

Tonight, after drinking too much wine
and watching a film about finding a body

not exactly Christ, I watered the fern.
An invisible bird flew out of the leaves

against my face. I kept watering,
listening, took a walk around the block.

Later, washing up, I noticed bird droppings
on my arms. I washed them off slowly,

reverently. Like I was doing
something holy for a change.

Closing In

More & more needles fall from the pines.
Everywhere symbols, if that's your thing.
To live always in the possible, to urge
your flesh to be as keen as melons softening
on summersad vines. I am tired of everything
that isn't lovely. I am tired of the way my
shoulders hoard stress, stacks & stupid stacks.
Everybody's an expert in somebody else's
business. I do not want to be any busier
than my basil plant, swallowing the sun,
the soil, the errant water. We suppose we
know a thing or two about botany, about
the intelligence of leaf, stem, root. Have you
noticed the way plants lean, as though longing
for news from a neighbor, a song, a touch, just
a little touch. It has been
a hard season for bodies, for the given
strangeness of care. Even now, the kind
music of a lark lingering in the crape myrtle
has something bereft about it. Like a whistle,
moving through lips, sounds going &
coming, the desirer closing in on the desired.

STANLEY KUNITZ

Touch Me

Summer is late, my heart.
Words plucked out of the air
some forty years ago
when I was wild with love
and torn almost in two
scatter like leaves this night
of whistling wind and rain.
It is my heart that's late,
it is my song that's flown.
Outdoors all afternoon
under a gunmetal sky
staking my garden down,
I kneeled to the crickets trilling
underfoot as if about
to burst from their crusty shells;
and like a child again
marveled to hear so clear
and brave a music pour
from such a small machine.
What makes the engine go?
Desire, desire, desire.
The longing for the dance
stirs in the buried life.
One season only,
                and it's done.

So let the battered old willow
thrash against the windowpanes
and the house timbers creak.
Darling, do you remember
the man you married?
Touch me,
remind me who I am.

Being & Waiting

So much of the past
drifts back with them—
cherry blossoms

—BASHO

BRENDA HILLMAN

REACHING PAST THE HUMAN

My poetic practices in this human existence are influenced by a variety of mythic, naturalist, scientific, and historical models. I have talked to plants since childhood because my mother talked to plants and her mother did before her; it seemed a smart thing to do to reach out past the human species. Talking to plants is not mere animistic wish fulfillment; it stems from a sense that whatever experience the plants are having is adjacent to our own, and that there are, between our physical outlines, some liminal spaces for play, places to create something more than humanistic projections.

In childhood, I talked to plants because I sympathized with them, stuck in their pots or soil, unable to walk away. Now I talk to them with a bit of poetic performance or ritual, even in secret. Though I have no idea if "experience" is the right word, I would like the plants to experience what I am able to offer as I try to take back some of the harm my human footprint might have caused on the planet.

Brenda's Garden Greens

- Go out to garden if you have a garden or to the market if you don't.

- Check to see what is coming up and not eaten by aphids.

- Gather a combination of greens: small kale leaves, small collards, the red-veined Japanese green that Luke planted, some mustard greens—not too many, they are peppery—and arugula, or dandelion greens (our chard tends to get bugs so we stopped trying).

- Talk to the rest of the plants encouragingly in whatever language or tone you use for the purpose.

- Take the cut ones inside, rinse them off, save the water in a bucket to carry back out to the garden.

- Sauté a lot of garlic (at least ½ tablespoon) in 2 or more tablespoons olive oil; add lots of shallots chopped up.

- When they are limp, add your greens to the pan.

- Decide whether you want to eat them bright green and a bit crunchy (in which case stir them with a wooden spoon for 5 minutes or so) or stewed a long time (in which case you can add some broth and cover for 1 to 2 hours).

ROBERT HASS

Levitation

A hummingbird lights on a woody stem of the cantua,
perches there stilled and looks around. An Anna's,
the feathers on its neck catching the light
as it moves its head in the jerky motions
of a movie dinosaur and tilts its beak toward the sky,
the gesture of humans who think well of themselves,
though I think the bird might be thinking about ants
or small spiders. Or maybe it is just taking the air.
It's late June. The morning had been foggy, marine mist
blowing in from the Pacific in billowing gusts,
so it is only now in the early evening that the fog
has burned off and the summer air settled in.
Maybe the bird is watching whatever interests it
in the same way that I am watching the bird.
The flowers of the cantua withered weeks ago,
the cascade of scarlet trumpets that seem to have been made
for hummingbirds (which means that they were made
by hummingbirds) dangle down in small, shriveled clusters.
The white flowers of the climbing rose have also withered.
Floribunda: the creamy blossoms so abundant on the trellis
I didn't like to cut bunches of them to take inside,
though I knew, of course, that they die one way
or the other, in the house or on the vine. The hydrangea
has only just begun to blossom, the clusters
of their flowers a white tinged faintly with pale green.

Also the fuchsia with its slim, graceful, pale pink flowers
is just beginning to bloom. There are clocks in seeds,
the one that turned off the cantua and the one
that turned on the hydrangea. And the hummingbird's heart
is a clock. Mine, too. When I look up from registering this fact,
it is gone. Probably working the nectar in the fuchsias,
wings beating so rapidly they almost seem not to be there.

STEPHANIE BURT

Love Poem with Horticulture and Anxiety

Ever imagine we might be garden gnomes?
        Not the beards or the caps but the aspect of hiding together,
up to our red boots in loamy topsoil, attentive
                to buds in the rain, saying spells that might let them grow
                stronger,
giving occult encouragement to our ground
                cherries, grape tomatoes on trellises,
pickling cucumbers, wallflowers, helical vines.
        The longer we stand, the more the wooden
soil-boxes feel like palaces,
                the loam itself like food, and like fresh riverbed affines
in which, when sifted, grains of gold are found.
        My love, I am here with you amid the endive,
in the comedy of gardeners who may never
                know what's coming but dig in,
and shade our moderate crops, and do not isolate
                ourselves from regular sun.
Of course we have feet of clay,
        or fins. Of course we made promises—everyone does—
that we will alter together, but not today.
        We cherish our oversize shoes.

Our garden also has sylphs
        that only we can see, and peonies,
and badger tracks, and a sandstone Artemis,
        and colors not found in nature
except in flowerbeds: intense maroons. Deep golds. Sleek pinks. Warm blues.

Loveliest of Trees

Loveliest of trees, the cherry now
Is hung with bloom along the bough,
And stands about the woodland ride
Wearing white for Eastertide.

Now, of my threescore years and ten,
Twenty will not come again,
And take from seventy springs a score,
It only leaves me fifty more.

And since to look at things in bloom
Fifty springs are little room,
About the woodlands I will go
To see the cherry hung with snow.

Mississippi Invocation

Come, green, fill our veins
    with tendrils and broad lobed leaves,
        wave as the rain approaches, teach us
      the secret of swoon, exhaustion. Come,
great-petaled magnolias, scrotal figs
    in the crooks of branches, scarlet bells
        of Carolina creeper, bruised gardenias,
      mosses and lichens that fur the bark of
oaks. Come, fungi, come, buzzards,
      this teeming   is death   is teeming,
        the walls of our houses, the doors
      of our senses, dampen and soften.
Plunge us into sleep and deliquescence,
    we are sap and vine and solstice,
        ooze us, rot us, make us hot and hotter.
      Jasmine, wisteria, twine us, ensnare us,
stupefy us with your sugary blossoms.

JACQUELINE KOLOSOV

Quickening

Twenty weeks and two days

Amid the camaraderie of starlings, morning
ripens along with the tomatoes on the vine.
A single twist at the stem, and summer
falls into my hands, another garden's
perfume of lemon balm and sage
between my fingertips, my mother's
kerchiefed face. August ripens,
tornadoes lavishing beside currants'
fairytale orbs. Always, the robins
and the sparrows picnicked on the fattest
of the translucent fruit my mother,
with sandy cupfuls of sugar, simmered
into jam I spread on toast, sitting
barefoot and caramel-kneed beneath
the patio's canopy of sun. But tomatoes
we always ate fresh and whole.

For weeks now, you and I
have been eating tomatoes as if the harvest's
bounty will never cease. My breasts, too,
are tomato-heavy, the bowl of my belly
dense with the curve that will only continue
to deepen in the months ahead. Lingering
in bed this morning, I lay my hands
along the rise, palms and fingertips
listening for our daughter. *Quickening,*
the doctor called it, the desire
for the coming child. Imagine:
next August, we will carry our daughter
into the garden. We will hold
the fruit to her face;
we will teach her tomatoes.

CHIYUMA ELLIOTT

All else is pale echo, dear

What's in my locket, what's in my pocket,
what grows green from my left eye socket:

lock of hair   lint and house key   holly,
my love's a-building a garden folly,

my love's a bird, my love's a plea—
my love, meet me in the orangerie

with your fat watch ticking in a garden glove
and vermiculite spilling on the floor like proof,

like feed in a barn, pi squared over six,
my love, lend me twelve willow sticks,

unswear to put me on the shelf;
Midas, touch me—forget yourself.

FROM *Just Tell Them No*

Field flecked purple with nightshade
and lupine. Ruby-throated bird
at the bottle-brush bloom. One's
own mediocrity sharpens it.

To the Grackle

Indecent bird. Lovely
        as an oil slick with wings,
you've called me
        to the summer garden.

Tin cans of light are crashing
        through the pear tree—
trash, umbel, globe and bract,
        come kiss my ass—that's how

you sound, how you (rash bird!)
        can lure me. Can I keep coming back
to this garden, if I'm called?
        There's a man I love

and a boy, who will be a man,
        whose bones I still feel click
and thrash where I put my arms around him
        just this morning—The lash

of your voice tells me, I should call
        my loves while I can
to listen to the grackles croak and clack
        in a nest built with half a ramen cup.

They tumble out into the yard.
    For a moment, two tall figures
stand twitching like the stuck hands of a clock
    then, crude slash of sound—

boy or man (or you, bird)—sends them
    swooping and dashing through
panicles, perennials, old blackberry canes.
    Let it always be this way—noise

summoning, mustering us together
    to search out the brash
mother who curses
    and flashes her wings.

ARTHUR SZE

Oasis

A tiny spider crawls across the lit screen
of a laptop: what does it make of the world?
Men chisel flagstone and form a stepped patio;
soon a "for sale" sign will hang at the street.
Sleeping on my back, I snore then turn
to my side; in the morning you hum before
showering. In the afternoon, long lines
of rain vanish before striking the ground,
but we are not distraught; a black morel
rises in a garden; orange blossoming daylilies
arc near a half-spherical stone fountain.
Water murmurs in the basin before it spills
over the edge; before morning spills over
the edge, sunrise makes lakes between clouds.

DAVID BAKER

Pocket Garden in the City

You would miss it if you were hurrying.
If you were harried or the day was drab.

It's tucked between two old brownstones, now
a defunct pet store, a popup for sneakers.

Take the stone path back. It's so narrow—
the leaning greenery like sticky sleeves,

sunflower above, like a lighthouse, the ocean
aroma of yellow hibiscus. But what are they doing.

Two cops, in the back corner, under a lime tree.
Hooded figure between them—what's your name.

You stand there and they stand there.
Snapdragon. Hollyhock. Day lilies ablaze.

The Practice of Talking to Plants

Mama & i, we talk to plants, for
we are short girls close to the ground
       & speech is the golden miracle—;
i learn to write while she says *honey* (making a fire-pouch
in the *y*) to a speckled
       banana whose existence is energy broth.
To limp chrysanthemums she says *Come on* & drops
      a Bayer aspirin in; i curve our letters near a *cholla*
      after it lent some needles to my leg—

We're not good relaxers, childhood & i,
    we suffer a leafy need while God is a missing
       hypotenuse. We'll not a dreaded dandelion meet
         before her voice arrives at low violets.
       In summer, when spicy seeds escape so fine
a pepper tree to make sashay for the lahn-ger-ay drawer,
we speak to spices they put on Jesus,
       those poor bright spices staring in the dark . . .
He hath numbered every hair on your head, she said,
       meaning she hath numbered the hairs . . .

when we are out with our strangeness
in the west—she in her desert, i on a mountain
crouching near *Lilium parvum*
with the same amount of frail our mother feels,
—it will be quiet for a while but syllables
are there: inside a leaf, a syllable,
inside a syllable, a door—

HANNAH FRIES

Insects with Long Childhoods

June bug, stag beetle, cicada—
three, seven, thirteen years as larvae

feasting underground in the gentle
rot of roots and castoffs, gone generations,

only a few weeks in the light
sharp as the blades of consciousness, incessant

buzz, cosmic background of loss
threaded through late summer's throbbing

days, lush nights, a brevity so full
it must feel like the eternity they came from.

I have a child who asks a question
of the air's every hum. He has not learned grief.

Sky, he says, and shovels soil into his mouth,
lets it drip out mud.

Gardeners' World, *or*
What I Did During the Plague

For that hour, only the earth
of his garden. Dark and friable
as chocolate cake, thronging
with nematodes and fungi,
more microbes in a spoon than humans
on the planet. A fear-free hour.
An hour without my trip-wired heart.
Were you aware the peony,
like the potato, is a tuber?
I was in love with his green
suspenders. I wanted to climb inside
his wellies and ample sweater,
weave fences out of willow sticks,
my old retriever dozing in the grass.
Outside my door lay California—
land of *exceptional* drought, abundant
fire. My own beds overrun
with want. And so, each night,
I watched a kind Englishman tend
gooseberries, exquisite crimson
dahlias, pale drifts of crocuses and snowdrops.
I learned how to harvest seeds, prune
a geranium, keep my rose bush blooming
all December. How to take cuttings
from my lilac so it would go on making
more of itself, its beauty and its sweetness.

Grieving & Release

. . . leaf subsides to leaf.
So Eden sank to grief,
So dawn goes down to day.
Nothing gold can stay.

—ROBERT FROST

DANUSHA LAMÉRIS

GRIEF & SUSTENANCE

Why do we grieve in gardens? The psychotherapist and former monk Thomas Moore once suggested that we each consider planting a garden to Saturn, a designated place to hold our melancholy and grief. I'm not sure what I would put in mine, but I imagine it to be mossy and secluded. And come to think of it, I did keep a small corner of a garden at my former home to go to when I needed to cry. It was fairly unadorned, just a pink camellia shrub against the house, and a stone lion's head, which hung from the tall wooden fence. No one could see me there. I could address my woes to the lion, which stared on, impassive and detached as I wished I could have been.

I was a mother of a child who would never walk, or talk, or speak—a trinity of omissions that felt, back then, almost unbearable. And worse, he would not live long. I'd buried his placenta under a lemon tree in the backyard. I'd watered too many hopes for him, my only child. And now, in some ways, his memory waters me, grows me into the unexpected self I keep becoming.

Rainbow Roasted Root Vegetables

In Barbados, where my mother was born, root vegetables are referred to as "ground provisions," a phrase I find both descriptive and charming. She told me that the island has had its share of centenarians, who when asked about the key to their longevity have referenced these provisions as a factor in their health and hardiness. These foods tie me to the strength of the people I come from, the lineage that passes through us all, unbroken. A roasted, earthy sweetness, despite our suffering. May whatever you have been through be transformed to sustenance by the fires of time and attention.

    2 or 3 beets, preferably in an assortment of colors
    A couple of turnips
    A yam
    A sweet potato—or two!
    A bunch of carrots (rainbow-colored a plus)
    A rutabaga (if you feel daring)
    3–4 tablespoons water
    A handful of rosemary, diced
    Salt and pepper

The first step, in any recipe, is to think of who you are cooking for and smile, sending them good wishes in advance. I am a firm believer in the alchemy of sharing food. Turn the oven to 375°F (190°C). Then you might put on some of your favorite music and sing along as you begin to cube all the vegetables. You might be the sort to peel the skins. I seldom do. I was taught the vitamins live in the outer layers, and, right or wrong, that has stayed with me.

At any rate, skins or no, cut them all into cubes of about a half inch to an inch at most. Then spread out all that gorgeous cut-up color on a large baking sheet, one with sides (unlike some cookie sheets). Add the water. Add the diced rosemary. Sprinkle on the salt and pepper. Cover with aluminum foil and put the sheet in the oven. Roast for about 30 minutes, then remove and uncover. Roast uncovered for another 15 to 20 minutes. Now, if everything has gone according to plan, they should be sweet and soft and almost exquisite! If not, cook a little longer till the magic happens.

Working in the Garden,
I Think of My Son

Who is nothing, now, but a few fistfuls of ash. Not even that, since ash
dissolves and is taken into the bodies of plants, or swept into the air
on the wind. He's so very fine he slips undetected
through a whale's baleen, or a beetle's gullet. He can even rise
through a stalk of grass with the upward pull of phloem,
in these first green days of spring. He has no use, now, for the soft
black hair through which I would run a slender comb,
nor for his oddly shaped thumbs. Nor anything in this world.
Though the things of the world may have use of him,
his molecules filtering through them—carbon, oxygen, nitrogen,
a whisper of hydrogen—the modest building blocks of life,
quietly, and without announcement.

ILYA KAMINSKY

After Her Funeral, I Became an Environmentalist

I love the planet because
my Mother is in it.

I lie down and kiss
the earth's

pink balding forehead.

After All

Even when the garlic crop is good,
something else is always dying—

the peas withering in the afternoon we hoped
for rain instead of watering, the tomatoes

over-shaded. It should teach us something
about pathos or fate, but really

couldn't we have tried harder? Predicted
the week of heat when the spinach bolted?

The trouble with gardening
is there's rain and wind and sun to blame,

like the woman in the buffer zone
outside the clinic who spat at me and screamed

What kind of man is he to bring you here?
while I held your hand, and our daughter curled

in her crib at home with the sitter.
Afterward, I dozed against you

on a park bench overlooking the city
until I was ready to go back to work.

But that's not gardening.
And still there's the garlic—

those round, paper-skinned heads
you pulled this morning and carefully laid out

to dry on the driveway's warm flat bed
below our window.

ADA LIMÓN

Invasive

What's the thin break
inescapable, a sudden thud
on the porch, a phone
vibrating with panic on the nightstand?
Bury the broken thinking
in the backyard with the herbs. One
last time, I attempt to snuff out
the fig buttercup, the lesser celandine,
invasive and spreading down
the drainage ditch I call a creek
for a minor pleasure. I can
do nothing. I take the soil in
my clean fingers and to say
I weep is untrue, *weep* is too
musical a word. I heave
into the soil. You cannot die.
I just came to this life
again, alive in my silent way.
Last night I dreamt I could
only save one person by saying
their name and the exact
time and date. I choose you.

I am trying to kill the fig buttercup
the way I'm supposed to according
to the government website,
but right now there's a bee on it.
Yellow on yellow, two things
radiating life. I need them both
to go on living.

CAMILLE T. DUNGY

Metaphor of America as This Homegrown Painted Lady Chrysalis

My head has come off
and by a string of my own creation
       is dragged what remains
of my last meal. Here, too, you see
my waste, and my brothers' and sisters'.
       You can take this literally or not.
Whatever I might have been has dissolved.
       When you moved me, I shook
       like a leaf preparing for autumn.
The child panicked. But soon, I returned
       to my patience. Call it potential
if you're feeling optimistic. There will be wings.
Bright, brown, black. With just a little
       white to set things off.

Palestine Vine

Seeds wrapped tenderly in plastic—
one package said *White*, one *Red*.

Hand-lettered, mailed by friends
I never met.

They grew instantly.
Strangely confining themselves to one corner

of the metal container, as if a metaphor.
I swear I planted them all over.

Leafy vines popped forth,
glory and green lengthening overnight.

I didn't notice one had twined around the rungs of the table.
Today, moving the pot, the biggest vine ripped out, broke off.

No! How could I have missed the simple
wrapping of the tendril suggesting happiness

in that exact light?
Its roots remain. A broken stem.

I wasn't evil, but I wasn't careful.
This is what happens in the world.

Now, soaking snipped vine in a glass of water, feeling
the hope and weight of so many years.

SHOLEH WOLPÉ

The Tulips of Tehran

The tulip garden north of the city is in bloom.
From the adjacent ground come the sounds of bickering,
laughter, shouts of children.

In a month, they will all be
dead, the tulips—but now they stand
tall on slim green stalks, flash fancy reds,
pinks and pearls. And the children?

By dusk
they'll be back in their little homes, eating dinner, watching
the country crumble on TV. This is the story of this
garden, not of the children or the holy war they will soon have to fight.

The tulips shiver and wait for now
and the damp soil swells with diligent worms.
The garden bows before its own god;
it will not believe in what cannot return.

SUSAN NGUYEN

Unending

I am learning how to hold grief
in my mouth. Something alive

until it isn't. Like a field is a field
until it isn't, until it is just the color green.

Listen when I tell you how a field
folds into a clover when I am on my hands,

how the memory of what I am looking
for is not as important as the ground

it claims. I don't mean that grief
can be unalive. Or that I keep it loaded

in that place between lower lip
and teeth. I mean I never walked the land

where my father harvested seeds.
In his field, he waited for green

to bend into gold. A single blade
splitting light until there was nothing else.

My father remembers. I watch my shadow.

MARY JO SALTER

Aloe

Somewhere between the store
where I'd bought the aloe plant
and its home arrival,

one waxen, prickly spear
had been rent in half.
Why leave a dead thing dangling

by a string? I snapped it off.
A pearly unguent oozed
into my palm, as if

I were the one bruised.
Well, if it thought so, sure.
I rubbed it in my skin.

So rough: I hadn't taken
care in so long . . . And why
hadn't I cried for help?

In the morning, a fresh ally
by instinct with itself,
the aloe had sealed up

its broken fingertip—
a low, but unbowed beauty
in its handicap.

My hand, not soft, was softer.
Well then, healing aloe?
Something to allow?

My Mother Is a Garden

In the backyard, my mother plants strands of razzleberry
fringe flowers. Next door the chartreuse golden feather
fare well. Before I am born, my mother is acquired
by the United States—coerced by some American
zodiac dream she fled to Los Angeles and decades later
she still withholds from speaking English, and only fertile
names of flowers have taken root. She is luminous. Her hair,
a blackish grey against the philodendron, long and parted
in the center. I lose her in the shade of overgrown impatiens
hanging onto the hillside behind the house. The horizon waves
in lines of barberry and nettles, silver waves of wild deer grass.
I have not spoken to my mother in years. Today I surprise her
with a visit and in the window's glow I watch her work.
I have taken the shape of her hips.

FROM *Song of Myself*

The spotted hawk swoops by and accuses me, he complains of my gab
      and my loitering.

I too am not a bit tamed, I too am untranslatable,
I sound my barbaric yawp over the roofs of the world.

The last scud of day holds back for me,
It flings my likeness after the rest and true as any on the shadow'd
wilds,

It coaxes me to the vapor and the dusk.

I depart as air, I shake my white locks at the runaway sun,
I effuse my flesh in eddies, and drift it in lacy jags.

I bequeath myself to the dirt to grow from the grass I love,
If you want me again look for me under your boot-soles.

You will hardly know who I am or what I mean,
But I shall be good health to you nevertheless,
And filter and fibre your blood.

Failing to fetch me at first keep encouraged,
Missing me one place search another,
I stop somewhere waiting for you.

DAVID BIESPIEL

Laurelhurst

Green on yellow
Wings along the hedges, the arrow-sharp
Leaves, or along the low, silver fences,
Along bark and sawed limbs and stray crows.
Everything a little-late-May-still-wet,
Full hour from last light,
Then splotches, then ash
Of stars in the milling, rich, wet
Silica sponge of the sky.
The moment I can taste the rain
Gurgling in the air, the gray
Paste of clouds through the tree limbs,
Like a wash or a stain,
I'm sitting in the kitchen-
Dark, at the formica table,
Short of breath, my grief as large
As a son's. Alone in such an hour
My body is a scar aching behind my neck.
Patch of green lawn, newly
Planted corn, tomatoes, wayside
Compost deep in the ground—
The day I dug out the garden
I felt like weeping, and later, in bed,
Watching the sky pass inside the
Open windows, I slept

Crooked as a feather.
In dogs asleep on the floor,
In metal wisp of stars,
In wind in the window sashes,
I remember white roses,
Lapping of water in a silver bowl,
Silver and red tomato cages,
Blue planters. The season
Bleeds with it.

Harvest & Feeding

Soil for legs
Axe for hands
Flowers for eyes
Bird for ears
Mushroom for nose
Smile for mouth
Songs for lungs
Sweat for skin
Just enough

—NANAO SAKAKI

ELLEN BASS

OF FOOD & PHYSICAL HOURS

Some years ago when our son was farming in Santa Rosa, a few hours north of our home in Santa Cruz, I drove up to help him with the harvest. My wife was with her sister who was in a coma in Portland on an ECMO machine that pumped blood out of her body, removed the carbon dioxide, and sent the oxygen-filled blood back in. The longer you're on the machine, the higher the death rate. My sister-in-law had been on longer than anyone working in that hospital could remember.

As the day wore on, my wife kept calling with more and more dire reports. There was nothing we could do, so we continued to pick string beans, dig up beets, carry melons in the heat. By the time I started cutting the tall black-eyed Susans for the farmers' market, the sun was low in the sky and blinding. When my wife called again, our son took the phone and told her to come home. We'd been holding off, but we now had to tell my wife's mother that her daughter might die.

And then, she lived. She is well. I don't know if being in the field helped me get through the day, but the physicality of those hours embedded itself in my memory—the dirt, the plants, the heat, the sweat, that relentless sun.

Melon & Cucumber Gazpacho with Basil Oil

After my sister-in-law's recovery, for our son's birthday we took him to Flea Street Café in Menlo Park, California, where we ate melon and cucumber gazpacho. Both my wife and our son are excellent cooks. I am not, but we loved this soup so much that I joined my wife in trying to replicate this delicious soup at home. This is the first—and perhaps only—recipe that I've had a hand in creating. It's very easy and very fancy, and it's exquisite on a warm day. You can serve it as an appetizer or by itself with a loaf of crusty bread. You can use any green-fleshed melon. We like honeydew, but you could also do a combination of honeydew and casaba. Bon appétit!

GAZPACHO

- 1 melon
- 2 cucumbers
- 2½ tablespoons ricotta cheese
- 3 teaspoons white wine vinegar
- 3 tablespoons good olive oil
  Juice from 1 lime
- 1 teaspoon salt

Peel, seed, and cube the melon and cucumbers. In a blender or food processor, or using an immersion blender, purée the melon with the other ingredients until smooth. And there you have your gazpacho! Put it in the refrigerator to chill.

BASIL OIL

- 1½ cups (packed) fresh basil leaves
- ¾ cup olive oil

The basil oil takes this gazpacho from terrific to out of this world. Blanch the basil in a saucepan of boiling water for 10 seconds. Then quickly drain and rinse it under cold water. Pat the basil dry with a clean dish towel or paper towels. In a blender or food processor, combine the basil with the oil. Transfer the mixture to a small bowl and let it stand for 30 minutes. Then strain it through cheesecloth. Some folks say you can make this oil days ahead, but we found it loses its flavor quickly and it's best to make it and serve it the same day.

To serve, pour soup into bowls and then drizzle a little basil oil on the top.

Apricot

A summer Taos sunset in your hand.
The weight of a small child's fist,
a girl, resisting sleep
as she sleeps.
The shape of a chicken angel's egg.
Eros's lovely clefted backside
in velvet. Fleshy
as a horse's lazy, lower lip.
A faraway fragrance:
juniper in gin, that slow gin
kiss.
What God saw on the eighth day, and ate, and said of it—
way good.
The woody stone we worry-gnaw when death's near,
when we're toothless again as babies,
trying to keep a great thought
small.

JANE HIRSHFIELD

Speed and Perfection

How quickly the season of apricots is over—
a single night's wind is enough.
I kneel on the ground, lifting one, then the next.
Eating those I can, before the bruises appear.

W. S. MERWIN

Black Cherries

Late in May as the light lengthens
toward summer the young goldfinches
flutter down through the day for the first time
to find themselves among fallen petals
cradling their day's colors in the day's shadows
of the garden beside the old house
after a cold spring with no rain
not a sound comes from the empty village
as I stand eating the black cherries
from the loaded branches above me
saying to myself Remember this

More

I know it's summer when we wade out
into the field and pick these crisp wonders,
tiny cucumbers bleached of their green
as if they've already seen too much
of this dazzling light, and can take no more.
We eat them sprinkled with salt and pepper,
as their name suggests, crunching through
flesh so sweet it's like that of a melon.
I've never seen them for sale in grocery stores,
but they grow here in this soil out of which
my husband could coax almost anything
with his sure touch and sharp attention.
He snaps them from stems with flowers still
shriveled at the ends, then hands them to me
like the gifts they are, and I take each one
into the bowl of my hands, a wandering monk
finally at home among rolling mountains
swaddled in trees, and stones heaved up
as round as eggs from sandy loam. So much
already alive between us, so many blessings
threading our days like the gold of sun,
yet here I stand, holding this bounty,
begging for more.

JAMES CREWS

ABUNDANT BLESSINGS

Living in cities and moving from place to place for most of my adult life, I had fallen out of the habit of gardening. Like many, I'd lost touch with the food I found for sale in grocery stores and even at farmers' markets, forgetting the pleasure (and intense hard work) of being part of the growing process from beginning to end. It wasn't until I moved to Vermont to live with my husband, an organic farmer, that I started feeling again what it was like to grow food and look after the land. Each summer day, I walked among the rows of farm fields with him, letting him teach me the names of all the vegetables, and harvesting what we needed for dinner—salad greens, heirloom tomatoes (Cherokee Purples became my favorite), basil, cilantro, and those crisp wonders, the salt and pepper cucumbers.

These walks reminded me of the gardens my father used to plant in our yard no matter where we lived, and I recalled how excited my brother and I felt every summer, to run out to our small plot and check on the progress of the carrots, zucchini, and cucumber plants growing wild in the unrelenting Missouri sun. Living close to the land has returned me to the pleasures of being rooted in a single place, and has instilled in me a sense of gratitude for the work of those who grow our food. Whether you're caring for a garden or tending to an entire farm, you can't stray too far without ensuring that someone's there to care for the plants you've been tending, and to receive the blessing of their bounty.

Salt and Pepper Cucumber & Heirloom Tomato Salad

This simple summer salad is all about allowing the flavors of the season to dominate.

- 8 salt and pepper cucumbers
- Salt and pepper
- 4 large heirloom tomatoes
- ¼ cup chopped basil
- ½ cup crumbled goat cheese
- 1 tablespoon balsamic vinegar
- 1 tablespoon olive oil

Chop the salt and pepper cucumbers into small cubes, sprinkling liberally with salt and pepper (as the name suggests) to bring out their sweet, melonlike taste. Cut the heirloom tomatoes into cubes (heirlooms tend to be meatier), and mix the cucumbers and tomatoes in a large bowl. Stir in the basil, then scatter the goat cheese over the top (fresh feta makes a nice substitute and adds a bit more saltiness to the salad). Next, drizzle in the balsamic vinegar, stir the salad, and add the olive oil. This salad pairs well with grilled meats and fish, and with an appetizer of bruschetta.

ELLEN BASS

Ode to the First Peach

Only one insect has feasted here—
a clear stub of resin
plugs the scar. And the hollow
where the stem was severed
shines with juice.
The fur still silvered
like a caul. Even
in the next minute,
the hairs will darken,
turn more golden in my palm.
Heavier, this flesh,
than you would imagine,
like the sudden
weight of a newborn.
Oh what a marriage
of citron and blush!
It could be a planet
reflected through a hall
of mirrors. Or
what a swan becomes
when a fairy shoots it
from the sky at dawn.

At the beginning of the world,
when the first dense pith
was ravished and the stars
were not yet lustrous
coins fallen from the
pockets of night,
who could have dreamed
this would be curried
from the chaos?
Scent of morning and sugar,
bruise and hunger.
Silent, swollen, clefted life,
remnant always remaking itself
out of that first flaming ripeness.

KATIE PETERSON

Fruit

He reaches his hand inside the tangle
to get the best ones out. Do I think they're the best
because they're the most hidden? Of course. Is there
philosophy in that? He thinks so. I can't see
how it would hurt. Ripening in the heat
of August. Orange and red and yellow. If these
small ones, these ones called *cherries*
were not called *tomatoes*
and were another word, I think that word
would be *bite*. I think I would like
being inside that tangle
of different varieties of plant. Not knowing
which one was called *celebrity* but knowing
it was there. My bones might stop being bones
and turn to something else. I ask him
if he has ever thought of that. I ask him just
that first part, before the reverie. He hasn't. I can't see
how it would hurt. I am forcing my hands
between two stems, just as he does and without
looking finding an orange one
that has yet to split its side and make
a wound of water with a seed
or two welling up to the surface, sometimes a whole line
of seeds like soldiers guarding this sweet

Equator of a border. I do this
because I have seen him do this. If there
was ever knowledge in me, I let it go
as I let the fruit go now, the one
we do not like to call a fruit. I let it go into this basket,
into this abundance, starting all over
with him again, as much because he likes it as because
all of it needs to be done.

KEETJE KUIPERS

After the Farmers Market, I Make a Salade Niçoise

The fingerlings slip, faded yellow pearls,
from my palms. Purple pole beans and flax wax—

I slice them down their slender lengths, blanched
now into brightness. Then a sack of dun

olives, oil-shined and speckled with scarce thyme,
precious as a clutch of glossed tanager eggs.

Just one small packet of smoked black cod—rich,
musky—gifted me from the frozen gut

of an Alaskan fishing boat. At last,
I crack delicate shells, pull something poached

and trembling from the water's curled lip.
The loose-limbed teens who sold me my vegetables—

not so much younger than myself, and yet
young enough I might once have made them—

could only have spent last night crushing
zucchini blossoms, fucking under fired

stars, their bodies and the last fleshy hours
of another day ripening beyond

all recognition, the reaped and the wasted,
in this shallow bowl where we lay it all.

Sous-Chef

I like cutting the cucumber, the knife slicing the darkness
into almost-transparent moons, each
with its own thin rim of night. I like smashing
the garlic with the flat of steel
and peeling the sticky, papery skin from the clove.
Tell me what to do. I'm free of will.
I carve the lamb into one-inch cubes.
I don't use a ruler, but I'd be happy to.
Give me a tomato bright as a parrot.
Give me peaches like burning clouds.
I'll pare those globes until dawn. The syrup
will linger on my fingers like your scent.
Let me escape my own insistence.
I am the bee feeding the queen.
Show me how you want
the tart glazed. I still have opinions,
but I don't believe in them.
Let me fillet the supple bones from the fish.
Let me pit the cherries. Husk the corn.
You say how much cinnamon
to spice the stew. I've made bad decisions,
so I'm grateful for this yoke
lowered onto my shoulders, potatoes
mounded before me.

With all that's destroyed, look
how the world still yields a golden pear.
Freckled and floral, a shimmering marvel.
It rests in my palm so heavily, perfectly.
Somewhere there is hunger. Somewhere, fear.
But here the chopping block is solid. My blade sharp.

Interview with the Pear Tree

When did you start making pears?

What is a pear?

(She runs her fingers over one
hanging on the branch.)

> *Mmm. Yes. It began*
> *before I could be seen,*
> *when the great body rang,*
> *striking, for the first time, the earth.*
> *Over the long day, it lay in the sun,*
> *and the birds came, and the flesh*
> *fell away until all that was left*
> *was the seed. Maybe it was*
> *when the moon swelled*
> *the seed, maybe*
> *when the first true*
> *leaf quickened.*

Did you always know you would make pears?

I wouldn't know how not to.

What is your process?

> *I let the leaves*
> *come to the branch*
> *and when the bee is at the*
> *blossom, I listen.*

Is dormancy difficult?

> *Dormancy?*

A period when nothing happens.

> *(The tree pauses.)*
> *I've never had one.*

What about drought?

> *I spread my root hairs and wait.*

Do you ever doubt?

> *When the bud breaks the green wood.*

Do you ever think of making apples?

What is an apple?

Could you describe the kind of pears you make?

(A ripe pear drops into her upturned hands.)

August

August.
The opposing
of peach and sugar,
and the sun inside the afternoon
like the stone in the fruit.

The ear of corn keeps
its laughter intact, yellow and firm.

August.
The little boys eat
brown bread and delicious moon.

To Autumn

Season of mists and mellow fruitfulness,
  Close bosom-friend of the maturing sun;
Conspiring with him how to load and bless
  With fruit the vines that round the thatch-eves run;
To bend with apples the moss'd cottage-trees,
  And fill all fruit with ripeness to the core;
    To swell the gourd, and plump the hazel shells
  With a sweet kernel; to set budding more,
And still more, later flowers for the bees,
Until they think warm days will never cease,
    For summer has o'er-brimm'd their clammy cells.

Who hath not seen thee oft amid thy store?
  Sometimes whoever seeks abroad may find
Thee sitting careless on a granary floor,
  Thy hair soft-lifted by the winnowing wind;
Or on a half-reap'd furrow sound asleep,
  Drows'd with the fume of poppies, while thy hook
    Spares the next swath and all its twined flowers:
And sometimes like a gleaner thou dost keep
  Steady thy laden head across a brook;
  Or by a cyder-press, with patient look,
    Thou watchest the last oozings hours by hours.

Where are the songs of spring? Ay, where are they?
  Think not of them, thou hast thy music too,—
While barred clouds bloom the soft-dying day,
  And touch the stubble-plains with rosy hue;
Then in a wailful choir the small gnats mourn
  Among the river sallows, borne aloft
    Or sinking as the light wind lives or dies;
And full-grown lambs loud bleat from hilly bourn;
  Hedge-crickets sing; and now with treble soft
  The red-breast whistles from a garden-croft;
    And gathering swallows twitter in the skies.

Green Tomatoes in Fire Season

There is smoke in the air
when I go pick them.

I go despite panic, also because
inside I'll make chutney.

For an hour or so, I unlatch them.
It is late fall. They will not ripen.

Firm pale green skins,
fine-coated in ash.

Our fire season goes all autumn now,
though today's fire is not

yet near to us.
But the green tomatoes: I love their pale lobes.

Tonight, god-willing,
we will fry some with cornmeal & fish.

Inside the air purifier whirs:
I will boil them with molasses & raisin.

Jar them for friends & the winter.
Disaster, we say, meaning bad star.

These are good green stars,
this is also their season.

Mask on, I bend & bend to the vine:
I bend & salvage what I can.

LUCILLE CLIFTON

cutting greens

curling them around
i hold their bodies in obscene embrace
thinking of everything but kinship.
collards and kale
strain against each strange other
away from my kissmaking hand and
the iron bedpot.
the pot is black,
the cutting board is black,
my hand,
and just for a minute
the greens roll black under the knife,
and the kitchen twists dark on its spine
and I taste in my natural appetite
the bond of live things everywhere.

GARRETT HONGO

Who Among You Knows the Essence of Garlic?

Can your foreigner's nose smell mullets
roasting in a glaze of brown bean paste
and sprinkled with novas of sea salt?

Can you hear my grandmother
chant the mushroom's sutra?

Can you hear papayas crying
as they bleed in porcelain plates?

I'm telling you that the bamboo
slips long pliant shoots
of its myriad soft tongues
into your mouth that is full of oranges.

I'm saying that silver waterfalls
of bean threads will burst in hot oil
and stain your lips like zinc.

The marbled skin of the blue mackerel
works good for men. The purple oils
from its flesh perfume the tongues of women.

If you swallow them whole, rice cakes
soaking in a broth of coconut milk and brown sugar
will never leave the bottom of your stomach.

Flukes of giant black mushrooms
leap from their murky tubs
and strangle the toes of young carrots.

Broiling chickens ooze grease,
yellow tears of fat collect
and spatter in the smoking pot.

Soft ripe pears, blushing
on the kitchen window sill,
kneel like plump women
taking a long, luxurious shampoo,
and invite you to bite their hips.

Why not grab basketfuls of steaming noodles,
lush and slick as the hair of a fine lady,
and squeeze?

The shrimps, big as Portuguese thumbs,
stew among cut guavas, red onions,

ginger root, and rosemary in lemon juice,
the palm oil bubbling to the top,
breaking through layers and layers
of shredded coconut and sliced cashews.

Who among you knows the essence
of garlic and black lotus root,
of red and green peppers sizzling
among squads of oysters in the skillet,
of crushed ginger, fresh green onions,
and pale-blue rice wine simmering
in the stomach of a big red fish?

GARRETT HONGO

TASTING HOME

Fifty years ago, in Hauʻula, on the windward side of Oʻahu, my family gave a big homecoming party for me at the Crescent Diner on Kamehameha Highway. I was 19 and hadn't been back to Hawaiʻi since I was 10, when my parents moved us to Los Angeles. When I arrived at Honolulu Airport, the entire clan was waiting for me. My grandfather had assembled all the aunts and uncles and the cousins of all ages and put a trio of them together in a guitar and ʻukulele band. What song they sang I can't recall, but it moved me to tears.

My grandparents owned the diner, and they had closed it for the celebration. On a long wood counter by the cash register were trays of nuts, smoked octopus, dried squid, and bottles of Primo, a local beer. One of my aunts brought from the kitchen three long platters of a dish she had picked up from the chef at the hotel where she worked. This was poke (pronounced *POH-kay*), the Hawaiian raw-fish salad made with marlin and ahi (yellowfin) or aku (skipjack) tuna. Though I'd often eaten sashimi, poke was then completely new to me—delicious rubies of cubed fish dressed in light sesame oil, garnished with minced bits of reddish-brown seaweed and the ground centers of kukui nuts. For nearly every afternoon of my Christmas vacation, I ate poke while I played cards with the relatives and tipped back cool sips of Li Po sake or the Primo my aunt served it with. The taste was of the sea, of the wealth of the land, and of homecoming.

Garrett Hongo's Poke

I make my own version of poke now, here where I live in Oregon,
when the weather is good and hot. I drive over to Newman's,
my local fish market, and pick up some fresh kajiki marlin, which
I cut into cubes. I buy my seaweed pickled in a bottle from an
Asian food market, and I chop a small bunch with some white
onion and minced garlic, toss the garnish onto the cubed marlin
in a stainless-steel bowl, squeeze a teaspoon or two of fresh
wasabi onto it, and mix in splashes of tamari sauce. My marlin
poke, pink cubes and rectangles in a blue Vietri bowl, can
bring me back to a hand of family five-draw in Hau'ula and a
cousin's airport falsetto welcome song, or settle me in to a clear
and breezeless midsummer day in my new home in Oregon.

1¼ pounds best-quality cubed tuna or marlin
¼ cup white onion, minced
¼ cup scallions, minced
2–3 cloves garlic, minced
3 tablespoons reddish-brown seaweed (like limu kohu or ogo)
1 tablespoon ground kukui nuts (also known as candlenuts;
   broken and unsalted dry-roasted peanuts are okay to substitute)
2 teaspoons sesame oil
½ teaspoon coarse sea salt
1–2 teaspoons wasabi
1½ tablespoons tamari (or soy sauce)

Garlic

You rise from the garden
swinging a bulb
of garlic like a thurible

•

or a lantern. Here is
the small light,
its filament of purple,

•

you kept earthed all winter.
A censer, cloven
yet bundled together.

•

Later I peel the skin
from two fleshy moons
and crush them.

•

In the black skillet:
iron, sulphur, oil spitting
like a meteor shower.

•

With a sprig of parsley
between your teeth,
you breathe

•

in my ear, take me
firmly in
your hand.

•

Through the openwork
of your body
comes a pomander

•

of photons and water.
What passes through me
with a shudder: Time,

•

heat, a vision of a star
yanked free from the night,
dirty with loamy sky.

Carrot

Take all summer,
your ember

from the sun,
its walking meditation.

Store it in small
vaults of light

to keep
the rest of us

when winter seals
around each day.

We'll flicker
to the table.

We'll gather
to your orange flame.

Turnip Ode

Turnips white as November moons
smooth baby skin   chill corpses
ice rain falls in the roof as I chop you—

You are cold you are crop
are roast you are soup
are bred to last winters

feed cattle
                    & keep us this side of death
which is perhaps why the ancestors

carved you for their hallows,
lit skulls against dark:
You un-root for lantern season.

Outside is wet & vines tangle—
Inside I quarter & broil you with bacon:
Light us with fat. Become inner lamp.

Wintering & Turning Again

Roll on rivers; raise your hands
cities! I, a faithful son of the black earth,
shall return to the black earth.

—CZESŁAW MIŁOSZ

HOLDING THE SEASON IN OUR HANDS

Fifteen years ago, toward the end of my marriage, my then-husband built two gardens at our house. One was large and took up what is now a brick, backyard patio. The other was a small front-yard patch of dirt near the garage. I say "built" because he used cinder blocks to border the space. Aesthetically, I saw the gardens as an eyesore: makeshift raised beds that any toddler might trip over. But my ex loved the idea of gardening. He ordered dirt from the local garden shop, used his father's rusted wheelbarrow to haul the soil from driveway to garden, and picked out every lush plant, every fragrant herb. That year, we had an abundance of cherry and Roma tomatoes, peppers, lettuce, basil, and oregano.

By the next year, our marriage was on life support and the gardens seemed more like a chore than a space to cultivate. After he moved out, I went through the motions of tilling the rocky New England soil. I watered the garden weekly instead of daily, and the vegetables suffered for it. My thumbs are brown. As a single mother, maintaining that garden became one more thing to cross off the to-do list. To my surprise, oregano from the previous year began to grow in the front yard. Small clusters bordered the areas where the cement driveway ended and grass began. Every time I mowed the lawn, a peppery oregano scented the air. It always gave me pause, made me a little regretful for the marriage we neglected.

Oregano is not a fussy plant. It propagated in my yard years after I dismantled the original gardens. Even in the winter

months, the leafy herb was still there in small bunches. To pick it in winter was like holding the past season in my hands. Even our heavy Massachusetts snowstorms couldn't kill it. Eventually, the driveway was repaved into a two-car space, large enough for my son and his friends to play basketball. We lost that crop of oregano, and with it I let go of the hurts that came from ending a marriage.

In recent years I have gone back to gardening—a pandemic can make you rethink all your life choices. The kids and I decided to remake our outdoor space for friends and family to gather and connect when the weather allows. With that new back patio, I added a manageable garden space that became a greenscape— a place that truly reflected this new phase of our lives. And while tomatoes, peppers, and lettuce are mainstays, what I love most is growing fresh herbs.

My goal was simple: I swore I would not buy another grocery store herb only to watch it wither in the refrigerator because I couldn't use the entire bunch. Oregano, parsley, cilantro, rosemary, thyme, and mint thrive in containers. And what I could not have predicted all those years ago is how much my teenagers would come to love cooking and eating what we grow with our own hands. For my son to pull basil leaves for a homemade pizza, or my daughter to grab twigs of oregano for a pasta recipe she's trying for the first time, gives me great joy! Even in the coldest of months, there's nothing like the faint smell of oregano gracing my fingertips long after the meal has ended.

Lemon Herb Pasta

1   pound pasta
3   tablespoons olive oil
1   clove garlic, thinly sliced
1   teaspoon chili flakes
    Freshly ground black pepper
    Zest of 1 lemon
    Juice of ½–1 lemon
¼   cup freshly chopped herbs (oregano, parsley, basil, any herb will do)
2–3   ounces Parmesan cheese, grated
    Kosher salt

Bring a pot of water to a boil and add the pasta. (I like linguini, but use your favorite.) Stir the pasta after 1 minute to ensure it doesn't stick. Meanwhile, in a skillet, add the olive oil, garlic, chili flakes, and pepper. Sauté over low to medium heat for 30 seconds.

Just before the pasta is done, drain it, reserving ¼ cup of pasta water. Add the pasta to the skillet and give everything a toss. Stir over low heat, adding the lemon zest and juice to taste. Add another drizzle of olive oil, the herbs, and the Parmesan cheese. Stir until combined.

Finally, add the pasta water, a splash at a time, until the sauce is your desired consistency. If too thick, add more pasta water. If too thin, add more cheese. Season with salt. Serve the pasta garnished with extra cheese, chopped herbs, and grated lemon zest.

Mind Is Snow

Mind is snow
       falling out of the sky's
mouth   white
     is the color
        of a soul:

           white

              is

            winter's little   green
                truth

ROSANNA WARREN

Season Due

They are unforgiving and do not ask mercy, these last
of the season's flowers: chrysanthemums, brash
sultan dahlias a-nod

    in rain. It is
    September. Pansy
    freaked with jet be

damned: it takes this radiant bitterness to
stand, to take the throb of sky, now sky
is cold, falls bodily, assaults. In tangled

    conclave, spiky-
    leaved, they
    wait. The news

is fatal. Leaf by leaf, petal
by petal, they brazen out this chill
which has felled already gentler flowers and herbs

    and now probes
    these veins for a last
    mortal volley of

cadmium orange, magenta, a last acrid flood
of perfume that will drift in the air here once more,
yet once more, when these stubborn flowers have died.

MARK DOTY

In the Community Garden

It's almost over now,
late summer's accomplishment,
and I can stand face to face

with this music,
eye to seed-paved eye
with the sunflowers' architecture:

such muscular leaves,
the thick stems' surge.
Though some are still

shiningly confident,
others can barely
hold their heads up;

their great leaves wrap the stalks
like lowered shields. This one
shrugs its shoulders;

this one's in a rush
to be nothing but form.
Even at their zenith,

you could see beneath the gold
the end they'd come to.
So what's the use of elegy?

If their work
is this skyrocket passage
through the world,

is it mine to lament them?
Do you think they'd want
to bloom forever?

It's the trajectory they desire—
believe me, they do
desire, you could say they are

one intent, finally,
to be this leaping
green, this bronze haze

bending down. How could they stand
apart from themselves
and regret their passing,

when they are a field
of lifting and bowing faces,
faces ringed in flames?

MICHELLE GILLETT

Daffodils

Some effort of light keeps the dusk unfinished.
Lying on my back, stretching the leg muscle
tight from bending over flower beds
planting for a season I can only imagine—
All I see through the skylight is sky
And what moves over it, a v of geese,
A cloud, a leaf. These are all we need
Of memory: what passes through the firmament,
What the dead would see looking up
If time made no barrier between coming
And going. My mind keeps the afterimages—
Skein of birds, cloud, leaf, what my hands
Held before burying. Three hundred bulbs
Huddle under earth,
Three hundred odds against weather.
When the darkness takes over,
I close my eyes. Everything is just where I left it.

Sunday

I rip everything out—the rugged cabbage stumps,
frost-killed basil stalks, withered squash vines—
pull up stakes, unwind twine and, one-by-one,
lob rotten tomatoes onto the compost.

He plows it all back into earthy rows,
then scythes a patch of asters by the shed,
where, side-by-side,
we stack the wire cages for next year's crop.

If this land is the sermon, our hands in it
must be some kind of appeal.
The blue wheelbarrow full of onions—
friable amber skins—I cart to the barn,

leaving the south doors open wide,
knot an arm's-length of cord
over a peg in the rough pine wall
and in the dust-lit quiet, braid.

JANE HIRSHFIELD

November, Remembering Voltaire

In the evenings
I scrape my fingernails clean,
hunt through old catalogues for new seed,
oil workboots and shears.
This garden is no metaphor—
more a task that swallows you into itself,
earth using, as always, everything it can.
I lend myself to unpromising winter dirt
with leaf-mold and bulb,
plant into the oncoming cold.
Not that I ever thought
the philosopher meant to be taken literally,
but with no invented God overhead,
I conjure a stubborn faith in rotting
that ripens into soil,
in an old corm that rises steadily each spring:
not symbols, but reassurances,
like a mother's voice at bedtime reading a long-familiar book,
the known words barely listened to,
but joining, for all the nights of a life,
each world to the next.

CLEOPATRA MATHIS

On the Twelfth of March

I am finally quiet, listening
to the clumps of snow release the house,
the silence given over to ducks clattering
in the freed pond where they crouched for weeks
on snow-covered ice. This new snow falls
without heart to hold to limb or stone.
The earth has had what it can take
and wants to rise out of its old shell.
If I could, I too would create some beginning.
I would walk out into the white curtain
that hangs like a border between grief and forgetting
and let the snow gather again, flake by flake
building its tiny monuments on the blades of grass,
on each brown-scarred flower of the dogwood
ready to open like the palm of a hand.
I would let all things of the past merge
as one, as every substance of a field is covered
without detail. And I would say: it is all here
beneath me, unchanged yet hidden.
I would walk until the cold
made me a part of the closed ground,
until the crow in my heart rose.
Maybe then I'd want these furled March buds
that stubbornly bring themselves forth, the broken
calendula already opening. I'd accept
what it is I've left here, the cicatrice
gleaming beneath the snow.

Wild Oregano

Winter, with its sky the color of ash
and a fresh dusting of snow
on the windshields of New England,

and all I can think of is the oregano
we planted years ago in our shitty garden.
It comes back year after year, now deeper

and deeper into the lawn while my neighbor's lawn,
beyond fences, through the cracked driveway,
grows greener than clover with a scent

that reeks of summer. Like an anarchist
the oregano does its own thing, self-willed
and tenacious, intense and free.

There's something in this grass
worth saving, I think to myself,
this one-plant wrecking crew

encroaching on clover territory
in a shimmering wave of language,
of green-speak. Manifest destiny

of the suburban world. How strange it feels—
tending a happiness beyond memory
in the cold, hard soil of January.

The Garden

Even by the gate we could not see
The rows. Only gone stalks, the paving stones
Upturned, the reach of wild cherry, beech and ash

Over the rusted post as if to claim whatever
Rises as their own. Who moves first, decides:
Clear the root, the withered stem, the slash

To burn next season. Stakes of names
And faded packets piled, cast out
By the entrance as the plow waits

For us to make sense of each original
Harrow, tamp, or hardened mound. This year
Will be better; the mole and crow each to their corner

As the horse turns to watch you deep in the dirt
To start with the one good and simple seed.

DEREK SHEFFIELD

Moon Garden

"Nothing that is not there and the nothing that is."
—Wallace Stevens

All winter the squares of wire fence
keep nothing in and nothing out. No

life among mounds of snow, only
every night's alabaster glow growing

until the stars with stick bones
and quick tongues begin to turn

the glitter of their cold eyes
toward us. But then it is us turning

one morning to the window to see
the earth returned. Yes, we can breathe out there.

We can reach our hands into warming heaps
of soil and with a fat thumb press in a seed.

Say one that shines like a drop of black.
A flower, say. Say the sun.

To Every Thing There Is a Season

—Ecclesiastes 3:1–8

To every thing there is a season, and a time for every purpose under heaven: a time to be born, and a time to die; a time to plant, and a time to pluck up that which is planted; a time to kill, and a time to heal; a time to break down, and a time to build up; a time to weep, and a time to laugh; a time to mourn, and a time to dance; a time to throw away stones, and a time to gather stones together; a time to embrace, and a time to refrain from embracing; a time to get, and a time to lose; a time to keep, and a time to cast away; a time to rend, and a time to sew; a time to keep silence, and a time to speak; a time to love, and a time to hate; a time for war, and a time of peace.

Ghost Eden

Garden of rock.
Garden of brick and heather.
        Garden of cranes with their hands raised
as if they know the yellow answer:
        to gather together—safety in numbers.
Garden of drywall frames, holes for windows
        punched out like teeth. Garden of bar fights.
Garden of rubble and gaps,
        spectral for-sale signs knocked
from wooden posts, bleached down
        to numbers ending in gardens of overgrown lots.
We are falling into ruin, garden
        of scaffolding and shale and gravel—
give us back our peace: a half-built garden
        of theft, treasures hidden in darkness,
newspapers crumpled on subfloors telling us
        to hold fast to that which is good.
Garden of rebar and saplings with trunks
        encased in corrugated piping
because many animals can girdle
        a tree's bark quickly: deer, stray cats, rabbits.
Garden of Tyvek wrap loosed
        and flapping like a ship's sail
in the gales, in the sheeting storms.

Hanging laundry left out in the garden
past darkness, fruit from the tree
of humanness: socks, shirts, underpants.
Garden of long exposures, half-light, traces
that empty themselves in tire treads running
like ladders through red clay mud:
the dirt from which we are formed
and crushed and formed again.

Contributors

DAVID BAKER'S books include *Whale Fall* (W. W. Norton, 2022) and *Swift: New & Selected Poems* (W. W. Norton, 2019), as well as 11 more collections of poetry and six books of prose about poetry. His individual works appear in *American Poetry Review, Atlantic, The Nation, New York Times, New Yorker, Poetry, The Yale Review,* and others. He lives, teaches, and gardens in Granville, Ohio. *("Pocket Garden in the City,"* 97)

MATSUO BASHO (1644–1694) may well be the world's greatest writer of haiku verses. Though he served as a samurai in his youth, he abandoned this status to devote himself to poetry. He is the author of the haunting classic *The Narrow Road to the Deep North.* His verses are widely translated throughout the world. *(haiku,* 81)

ELLEN BASS'S most recent book is *Indigo* (Copper Canyon Press, 2020). Among her awards are fellowships from the Guggenheim Foundation, the NEA, the California Arts Council, three Pushcart Prizes, and the Lambda Literary Award. A chancellor of the Academy of American Poets, she teaches in the MFA program at Pacific University. She developed a popular virtual series, *Living Room Craft Talks,* available at ellenbass.com. *(Of Food & Physical Hours,* 124 / *"Ode to the First Peach,"* 132 / *"Sous-Chef,"* 138)

EVAN BAUER is a poet and translator from Santa Cruz, California. His poems have appeared in *Poetry Northwest, Nashville Review,* and elsewhere. He has worked and lived in both Japan and the US, and is currently based in Seattle, where he works as a translator at Nintendo of America. *(Basho translation,* 81)

WENDELL BERRY is the author of more than 30 books of poetry, essays, and novels. About his work, a reviewer for the *Christian Science Monitor* wrote: "Berry's poems shine with the gentle wisdom of a craftsman who has thought deeply about the paradoxical strangeness and wonder of life." Among his honors and awards are fellowships from the Guggenheim and Rockefeller Foundations, a Lannan Literary Award, and a grant from the National Endowment for the Arts. Wendell Berry lives on a farm in Port Royal, Kentucky. *(from "Prayers and Sayings of the Mad Farmer,"* 23)

DAVID BIESPIEL is a contributing writer at the *New Republic, New Yorker, Poetry,* and *Slate.* He is the author of a dozen books, including, most recently, *A Place of Exodus: Home, Memory, and Texas.* *("Laurelhurst,"* 120)

SOPHIE CABOT BLACK has three poetry collections from Graywolf Press: *The Misunderstanding of Nature,* which received the Poetry Society of America's First Book Award; *The Descent,* which received the 2005 Connecticut Book Award; and, most recently, *The Exchange.* Her poetry has appeared in numerous magazines, including the *Atlantic, New Republic, New Yorker,* and *Paris Review.* *("The Garden,"* 173)

JERICHO BROWN is author of *The Tradition,* for which he won the Pulitzer Prize. He is the recipient of fellowships from the Guggenheim Foundation, the Radcliffe Institute for Advanced Study at Harvard, and the National Endowment for the Arts, and he is the winner of the Whiting Award. Brown's first book, *Please,* won the American Book Award. His second book, *The New Testament,* won the Anisfield-Wolf Book Award. He is the director of the creative writing program and a professor at Emory University. *("Foreday in the Morning,"* 37)

STEPHANIE BURT is a professor of English at Harvard. Her latest book is *We Are Mermaids,* published by Graywolf Press. *("Love Poem with Horticulture and Anxiety,"* 86)

VICTORIA CHANG'S latest book of poetry is *The Trees Witness Everything* (Copper Canyon Press). Her nonfiction book, *Dear Memory* (Milkweed Editions), was published in 2021. *OBIT* (Copper Canyon Press, 2020), her prior book of poems, was named a *New York Times* Notable Book and a *TIME* Must-Read Book and received the *Los Angeles Times* Book Prize, the Anisfield-Wolf Book Award in Poetry, and the PEN/Voelcker Award. It was also longlisted for a National Book Award and named a finalist for the National Book Critics Circle Award and the Griffin International Poetry Prize. She has received a Guggenheim Fellowship, and lives in Los Angeles, where she teaches in Antioch's low-residency MFA Program. *("Spring Planting,"* 52)

ALAN CHAZARO is a Bay Area writer and teacher. His books, *This Is Not a Frank Ocean Cover Album* and *Piñata Theory*, are available through Black Lawrence Press. Follow his updates on Twitter and Instagram: @alan_chazaro. *("Photosynthesis: [Chinaka Hodge Hosts a Block Party]," 68)*

LUCILLE CLIFTON (1936–2010) was a prolific poet and author of children's books whose works resonate enormous humanity and moral dignity. The *New Yorker* praised her ability to write "physically small poems with enormous and profound inner worlds." During her lifetime, among many honors, she won the National Book Award and served as a chancellor of the Academy of American Poets. *("cutting greens," 148)*

PATTY CRANE is author of the poetry collections *Bell I Wake To* (Zone 3 Press, 2019) and *something flown* (Concrete Wolf, 2018), as well as *Bright Scythe* (Sarabande Books, 2015), translations of the poems by Swedish Nobel laureate Tomas Tranströmer. Her work has been widely published and supported by MacDowell fellowships. *("Mind Is Snow," 163 / "Sunday," 169)*

JAMES CREWS is editor of the best-selling anthology *How to Love the World,* featured on NPR's *Morning Edition,* as well as in the *Boston Globe* and *Washington Post.* He is also the author of four prizewinning collections of poetry: *The Book of What Stays, Telling My Father, Bluebird,* and *Every Waking Moment.* His poems have appeared in the *New York Times Magazine, Ploughshares,* and *The Sun.* Crews teaches in the Poetry of Resilience seminars, and lives with his husband in Shaftsbury, Vermont. To sign up for weekly poems and prompts, visit jamescrews.net. *("More," 129 / Abundant Blessings, 130)*

DIANA MARIE DELGADO'S first collection, *Tracing the Horse,* was a *New York Times* Noteworthy Pick and follows the coming-of-age of a young Chicana making sense of who she is amid a family and community weighted by violence and addiction. Delgado's latest project, *Like a Hammer Across the Page: Poets on Mass Incarceration in America,* is under contract with Haymarket. She is the literary director of the University of Arizona Poetry Center. *("Greenbriar Lane," 26)*

MARK DOTY is the author of nine books of poetry, including *Deep Lane* (2015); *Fire to Fire: New and Selected Poems*, which won the 2008 National Book Award; and *My Alexandria*, winner of the *Los Angeles Times* Book Prize, the National Book Critics Circle Award, and the T. S. Eliot Prize. He is also the author of four memoirs: the *New York Times* bestseller *Dog Years*, *What Is the Grass*, *Firebird*, and *Heaven's Coast*, as well as a book about craft and criticism, *The Art of Description: World Into Word*. Doty has received two NEA fellowships, Guggenheim and Rockefeller Foundation Fellowships, a Lila Wallace/Readers Digest Award, and the Witter Byner Prize. ("Deep Lane," 44 / "In the Community Garden," 166)

CAMILLE T. DUNGY is the author of four collections of poetry, most recently *Trophic Cascade*, and the essay collection *Guidebook to Relative Strangers: Journeys into Race, Motherhood, and History*, a finalist for the National Book Critics Circle Award. Dungy has edited poetry anthologies, including *Black Nature: Four Centuries of African American Nature Poetry* and *From the Fishouse*. Her poems have appeared in Best American Poetry, *The 100 Best African American Poems*, *Poetry*, *New Yorker*, and many other print and online venues. Dungy's honors include the 2021 Academy of American Poets Fellowship, a Guggenheim Fellowship, an American Book Award, two NAACP Image Award nominations, and fellowships from the NEA in both poetry and prose. Dungy is a University Distinguished Professor at Colorado State University. ("Metaphor of America as This Homegrown Painted Lady Chrysalis," 112)

ANDY EATON is the author of *Sprung Nocturne* (Lifeboat Press, 2016), and his poems appear in *Copper Nickel, Narrative, Ploughshares, The Tangerine*, and *The Yale Review*, among other places. Recipient of the Ploughshares Emerging Writer Award, his work has been supported by the University of Virginia, the Bread Loaf Writers' Conference, the Arts Council of Northern Ireland, and the Ireland Chair of Poetry. ("Autumn Blooming Cherry," 36)

CHIYUMA ELLIOTT is an associate professor of African American Studies at the University of California, Berkeley. She is an avid gardener who loves drought-tolerant roses, heirloom tomatoes, and every fern she's ever met. Her two noisy dogs—Radish and Barney—help her harvest strawberries, peas, collards, and kale. Chi is the author of four books of poetry, including *Blue in Green* (Chicago, 2021). ("All else is pale echo, dear," 92)

ANN FISHER-WIRTH is the author of seven books of poems, including *Paradise Is Jagged* (Terrapin Books, 2023), *The Bones of Winter Birds* (Terrapin Books, 2019), and *Mississippi*, a poetry/photography collaboration with Maude Schuyler Clay (Wings Press, 2018). With Laura-Gray Street, Ann coedited *The Ecopoetry Anthology* (Trinity University Press, 2013; third printing 2020). A senior fellow of the Black Earth Institute, she has had senior Fulbright Fellowships to Switzerland and Sweden and residencies at Djerassi, Hedgebrook, the Mesa Refuge, and Camac/France, and was 2017 Poet in Residence at Randolph College. Her poems and essays have received numerous awards, including a Mississippi Arts Commission poetry fellowship. She recently retired from the University of Mississippi. *(Tendrils of Life & Community, 62 / "Haecceitas," 66 / "Mississippi Invocation," 89)*

HANNAH FRIES is the author of the poetry collection *Little Terrarium* and the book *Being with Trees*. She was awarded a scholarship from the Bread Loaf Writers' Conference and has been nominated for the Pushcart Prize. Her work has appeared in *American Poetry Review, Massachusetts Review, EcoTheo Review, Terrain.org,* and other publications. She lives in western Massachusetts. *("Insects with Long Childhoods," 100)*

ROBERT FROST (1874–1963) was one of America's most beloved poets. The recipient of four Pulitzer Prizes, he was presented the Congressional Gold Medal in 1962. *(from "Nothing Gold Can Stay," 103)*

HALEH LIZA GAFORI is a poet, translator, vocalist, and educator born in New York City of Persian descent. Her translations of poems by the beloved Persian sage and mystic Rumi have been collected in the book *GOLD*, published by New York Review Books/NYRB Classics. Sharing her passion for the expansive, compassionate, and ecstatic nature of Rumi's poetry and philosophy, she both performs and teaches workshops at universities, festivals, and institutions across the country. *(Rumi translation, 21)*

FORREST GANDER, a writer and translator with degrees in geology and literature, was born in the Mojave Desert. Awarded the Pulitzer Prize and fellowships from the Guggenheim, Whiting, and United Artists foundations, Gander has most recently published *Knot*, a collaboration with Jack Shear, and *Twice Alive: An Ecology of Intimacies*. Gander translates books by poets from Spain, Latin America, and Japan. *(from "Just Tell Them No," 93)*

ROSS GAY is interested in joy. Ross Gay wants to understand joy. Ross Gay is curious about joy. Ross Gay studies joy. (*"A Small Needful Fact,"* 19)

MICHELLE GILLETT (1948–2016) lived in Stockbridge, Massachusetts, and was active in the art and literary communities of the Berkshires. She earned her MFA in poetry from the Warren Wilson College Program for Writers. Her collection *Coming About* was published in 2017 by Four Way Books. (*"Daffodils,"* 168)

MARIANA GOYCOECHEA is a writer and educator of Guatemalan-Argentinian descent based in New York City. Her work has been featured in *NYSAI Press*, *The Rumpus*, *Acentos Review*, Harvard's *PALABRITAS* magazine, *Fourth River*, *Selkie Lit Mag*, and, most recently, in *BreakBeat Poets Vol. 4: LatiNEXT*. She is a graduate of Ashland University's MFA program in poetry. (*"Palm Sunday,"* 67)

LEAH NAOMI GREEN is the author of *The More Extravagant Feast* (Graywolf Press, 2020), winner of the Walt Whitman Award from the Academy of American Poets. She received the 2021 Lucille Clifton Legacy Award and an AAP 2021 Treehouse Climate Action Poetry Prize. Green teaches environmental studies and English at Washington & Lee University. She and her family homestead in Virginia and grow much of their food for the year. (*"Carrot,"* 156)

THOM GUNN (1929–2004) was an English poet who was praised for his early verses in England. After relocating from England to San Francisco, Gunn wrote about gay-related topics—particularly in his most famous work, *The Man with Night Sweats*. He taught intermittently at the University of California, Berkeley. He is widely regarded as one of the twentieth century's great poets. (*"Considering the Snail,"* 50 / *"Fennel,"* 58)

ROBERT HASS is retired from the English department at the University of California, Berkeley. His most recent book is *Summer Snow: New Poems* (Ecco/HarperCollins). (*"Levitation,"* 84)

BRENDA HILLMAN'S eleventh collection of poetry, *In a Few Minutes Before Later*, was published by Wesleyan University Press in 2022. She served as a chancellor for the Academy of American Poets from 2016 to 2022 and lives in the San Francisco Bay Area where she is a professor emerita at Saint Mary's College of California. Learn more about her at blueflowerarts.com/artist/brenda-hillman. (*Reaching Past the Human,* 82 / *"The Practice of Talking to Plants,"* 98)

JANE HIRSHFIELD is the author of nine much-honored collections of poetry, most recently *Ledger* (Knopf, 2020), centered on the crises of biosphere and social justice. *The Asking: New and Selected Poems 1971–2023* will appear from Knopf in fall 2023. Her work appears in the *New Yorker, Atlantic, New York Times, Poetry,* and 10 editions of Best American Poetry. A former chancellor of the Academy of American Poets, she was elected in 2019 into the American Academy of Arts & Sciences. (*In Praise of Strong Seedlings,* 40 / *"The Contract,"* 54 / *"Speed and Perfection,"* 127 / *"November, Remembering Voltaire,"* 170)

GARRETT HONGO is the author of *Coral Road: Poems.* His most recent book is *The Perfect Sound: A Memoir in Stereo.* He teaches at the University of Oregon. (*"Who Among You Knows the Essence of Garlic?"* 149 / *Tasting Home,* 152)

GERARD MANLEY HOPKINS (1844–1889), a Jesuit priest, was one of the Victorian era's greatest poets and is known for innovating a metrical device known as sprung rhythm. (from *"Inversnaid,"* 39)

A. E. HOUSMAN (1859–1936) was a scholar of classics and the author of the enormously popular collection of poems *A Shropshire Lad.* (*"Loveliest of Trees,"* 88)

JACK JOHNSON was raised in Peshastin, Washington, a small town near the Cascade Range. He received his MA from Southern Illinois University and did postgraduate work at the University of Denver. Upon returning to Washington, he and his wife, Devera Sharp, built their home and raised two sons there. His book of poetry, *The Way We Came In,* was published in 2020 by Main Street Rag. He teaches English and philosophy at Wenatchee Valley College. (*"Stained Glass,"* 43)

ASHLEY M. JONES is poet laureate of the state of Alabama (2022–2026). She is the author of *Magic City Gospel* (Hub City Press, 2017), *dark / / thing* (Pleiades Press, 2019), and *REPARATIONS NOW!* (Hub City Press, 2021). She teaches creative writing at the Alabama School of Fine Arts and in the low-residency MFA program at Converse University. Jones codirects PEN

Birmingham, and she is the founding director of the Magic City Poetry Festival. She recently served as a guest editor for *Poetry* magazine, and she was a 2022 Academy of American Poets Poet Laureate Fellow. (*Becoming New & New Becoming*, 22 / "Photosynthesis," 24)

ILYA KAMINSKY, born in Odessa in the former Soviet Union, arrived in the US in 1993, when his family was granted asylum. He is the author of *Deaf Republic* (Graywolf Press) and *Dancing in Odessa* (Tupelo Press), and coeditor and cotranslator of many other books, including *Ecco Anthology of International Poetry* (Harper Collins). His work has won many awards, including a Guggenheim Fellowship, a Whiting Award, the American Academy of Arts and Letters' Metcalf Award, a Lannan Fellowship, and an Academy of American Poets' Fellowship, and has been shortlisted for the National Book Award, National Book Critics Circle Award, Neustadt International Literature Prize, and T. S. Eliot Prize. (*"After Her Funeral, I Became an Environmentalist,"* 107)

KIRUN KAPUR'S book, *Women in the Waiting Room,* was a finalist for the National Poetry Series and was published by Black Lawrence Press (2020). Kapur serves as the editor of the *Beloit Poetry Journal,* one of nation's oldest poetry publications, and teaches at Amherst College where she is the director of the creative writing program. She lives north of Boston with her family. To learn more, visit her at kirunkapur.com. (*"To the Grackle,"* 94)

JOHN KEATS (1795–1821) was a Romantic poet and friend of Lord Byron and Percy Bysshe Shelley. His poems had been in publication for less than four years when he died of tuberculosis in Rome. (*"To Autumn,"* 144 / "On the Grasshopper and Cricket," 200)

JACQUELINE KOLOSOV is the author of four poetry collections, most recently *Talons, Wings* (Salmon Poetry, 2023) and the story collection *Exit, Pursued by a Bear* (Hollywood Books, 2023). Originally from Chicago, she now lives, teaches, writes, and rides in West Texas where her daughter, now 16, occasionally eats tomatoes. (*"Quickening,"* 90)

KEETJE KUIPERS is the author of three collections: *Beautiful in the Mouth, The Keys to the Jail,* and *All Its Charms,* which includes poems published in both the Pushcart Prize and Best American Poetry anthologies. Previously a Stegner Fellow, Keetje currently lives with her wife and children in Missoula,

Montana, where she is editor of *Poetry Northwest,* and a board member at the National Book Critics Circle. (*"After the Farmers Market, I Make a Salade Niçoise,"* 136)

STANLEY KUNITZ (1905–2006) was an American poet and avid gardener. He was appointed Poet Laureate Consultant in Poetry to the Library of Congress twice, first in 1974 and then again in 2000. (*"Touch Me,"* 78)

DANUSHA LAMÉRIS is the author of *The Moons of August* (Autumn House, 2014) and *Bonfire Opera* (University of Pittsburgh Press, 2020), which won the Northern California Book Award in Poetry. Some of her work has been published in the Best American Poetry, *Orion, New York Times, American Poetry Review, Ploughshares, Tin House,* and *Prairie Schooner.* The recipient of the 2020 Lucille Clifton Legacy Award, she co-leads the Poetry of Resilience webinars and Hearthfire Writing Community with James Crews; was the 2018–2020 poet laureate of Santa Cruz County, California; and is on the faculty of Pacific University's low-residency MFA program. (*"Feeding the Worms,"* 51 / Grief & Sustenance, 104 / *"Working in the Garden, I Think of My Son,"* 106)

JANICE LEE is a Korean American writer, teacher, spiritual scholar, and shamanic healer. She is the author of seven books of fiction, creative non-fiction, and poetry, most recently *Imagine a Death* (Texas Review Press, 2021) and *Separation Anxiety* (CLASH Books, 2022). She currently lives in Portland, Oregon, where she is an assistant professor of creative writing at Portland State University. (from *"Separation Anxiety,"* 65)

GENINE LENTINE is the author of *Poses: An Essay Drawn from the Model* and the three chapbooks *Archaeopteryx, Found Dharma Talks,* and *Mr. Worthington's Beautiful Experiments on Splashes.* She is coauthor with Stanley Kunitz and photographer Marnie Crawford Samuelson of *The Wild Braid: A Poet Reflects on a Century in the Garden.* For writing workshops and one-on-one sessions, visit geninelentine.com. She lives in San Francisco where she tends a seaside garden. (*"Interview with the Pear Tree,"* 140)

DANA LEVIN'S most recent book is *Now Do You Know Where You Are* from Copper Canyon Press. She serves as Distinguished Writer in-Residence at Maryville University in Saint Louis. (*"Golden Poppy,"* 48)

ADA LIMÓN is the author of six books of poetry, including *The Carrying*, which won the National Book Critics Circle Award for Poetry in 2019. Limón is also the host of the critically acclaimed poetry podcast *The Slowdown*. Her most recent book of poems is *The Hurting Kind* (Milkweed Editions, 2022). *("Trying," 64 / "Invasive," 110)*

FEDERICO GARCÍA LORCA (1898–1936) was a Spanish poet, playwright, and theater director known for introducing futurism and surrealism to Spanish literature. He was murdered by Nationalist Forces at the beginning of the Spanish Civil War. *("August," 143)*

DAVID MALLET is an American singer-songwriter best known for his authorship of the "folk standard" composition "Garden Song." *(from "Garden Song," 61)*

CLEOPATRA MATHIS has published eight books, most recently *After the Body: Poems New and Selected* (Sarabande Books, 2020). Her many honors include a Guggenheim Fellowship, two fellowships from the National Endowment for the Arts, and two Pushcart Prizes. The founder of the creative writing program at Dartmouth College in 1982, she lives in Thetford, Vermont. *("Earth," 34 / "On the Twelfth of March," 171)*

ERIKA MEITNER is the author of six books of poems, including *Useful Junk* (BOA Editions, 2022) and *Holy Moly Carry Me* (BOA Editions, 2018), winner of the 2018 National Jewish Book Award and a finalist for the National Book Critics Circle Award in poetry. Her poems have appeared most recently in *New Yorker, Orion, Virginia Quarterly Review, New Republic, Poetry*, and elsewhere. Meitner is currently a professor of English and the MFA program director at the University of Wisconsin–Madison. You can find more about her at erikameitner.com. *("Ghost Eden," 176)*

W. S. MERWIN (1927–2019) wrote more than 50 books of poetry and prose, and produced many works in translation. Merwin received many honors, including the Pulitzer Prize for Poetry in 1971 and 2009, and the National Book Award for Poetry in 2005. In 2010, the Library of Congress named him the seventeenth United States poet laureate. *("Black Cherries," 128)*

CZESŁAW MIŁOSZ (1911–2004) was a Polish poet. He lived in the US after 1960, spent many years teaching at the University of California, Berkeley, and was awarded the Nobel Prize in Literature in 1980. (*"Gift,"* 74 / from *"Hymn,"* 159)

CLAUDIA MONPERE'S poems appear in many journals, including *New Ohio Review, Plume, Hunger Mountain, Cincinnati Review,* and *Ecotone.* Her creative nonfiction and fiction appear in the *Kenyon Review, River Teeth, Prairie Schooner, Smokelong Quarterly,* and *Creative Nonfiction.* She's a recipient of a Hedgebrook residency and teaches creative writing and first-year writing at Santa Clara University. (*"Mara Mara, Garden Child,"* 70)

LAUREN MOSELEY is the author of the poetry collection *Big Windows* (Carnegie Mellon University Press). Her poems have appeared in the Poem-a-Day series from the Academy of American Poets, as well as in the *Iowa Review, Electric Literature, Third Coast, On the Seawall, Copper Nickel, Pleiades,* and elsewhere. Lauren has received fellowships from Yaddo, the Virginia Center for the Creative Arts, Hewnoaks, and the Barbara Deming Memorial Fund. She lives in Durham, North Carolina. (*"Planting Inkberry Hollies During the Pandemic,"* 30)

JASON MYERS is an executive director of EcoTheo Collective and editor in chief of *EcoTheo Review.* A National Poetry Series finalist, his work has appeared in *Kenyon Review, Orion, Paris Review,* and elsewhere. He is a priest in the Episcopal Diocese of Texas and lives with his family in Houston. (*"Closing In,"* 77)

AIMEE NEZHUKUMATATHIL is the author of the *New York Times* bestselling essay collection *World of Wonders* and four collections of poetry. With Ross Gay, she authored the epistolary chapbook *Lace & Pyrite* (Get Fresh Publishing). She is professor of English in the MFA program at the University of Mississippi. (*Foreword: The Whole World, a Garden,* 8 / *"Spring (a conversation),"* 29)

SUSAN NGUYEN'S debut poetry collection, *Dear Diaspora,* won the 2020 Prairie Schooner Book Prize in Poetry and was published by the University of Nebraska Press in 2021. Nguyen's poetry is interested in the body: how geography, history, and trauma leave markers, both visible and invisible. Her hobbies, beyond reading and writing, include photography, zine-making, hiking, and otherwise being outdoors. (*"Unending,"* 115)

NAOMI SHIHAB NYE recently served as Young People's Poet Laureate (Poetry Foundation). She is a professor of creative writing at Texas State University. (*"Palestine Vine,"* 113)

JANUARY GILL O'NEIL is the author of *Rewilding* (2018), *Misery Islands* (2014), and *Underlife* (2009), all published by CavanKerry Press, and is an associate professor at Salem State University. From 2019 to 2020, she served as the John and Renée Grisham Writer-in-Residence at the University of Mississippi, Oxford. She lives with her two children in Beverly, Massachusetts. (*Holding the Season in Our Hands,* 160 / *"Wild Oregano,"* 172)

ELISE PASCHEN is the author of *The Nightlife, Bestiary, Infidelities* (winner of the Nicholas Roerich Poetry Prize), and *Houses: Coasts.* Her poems have appeared in *Poetry,* Best American Poetry, and *A Norton Anthology of Native Nations Poetry,* among other anthologies and magazines. She has also edited many anthologies, including, most recently, *The Eloquent Poem.* Paschen teaches in the MFA writing program at the School of the Art Institute of Chicago. (*"Trapeze,"* 31)

KATIE PETERSON is the author of five books of poetry, including the 2021 collection *Life in a Field.* Her 2019 collection, *A Piece of Good News,* was shortlisted for the Northern California Book Award. *Permission* was published in 2013 by New Issues Press. She lives in Berkeley, California, with her family, and directs the MFA program in creative writing at UC Davis. (*"Fruit,"* 134)

LIA PURPURA is the author of nine collections of essays, poems, and translations. A finalist for the National Book Critics Circle Award for *On Looking* (essays), her awards include Guggenheim, NEA, and Fulbright fellowships, as well as five Pushcart Prizes. Her work appears in the *New Yorker, New Republic, Orion, Paris Review, Emergence,* and elsewhere. She lives in Baltimore, Maryland, where she is writer-in-residence at the University of Maryland, Baltimore County. (*"Weed,"* 42)

RUBEN QUESADA is the editor of a hybrid collection of essays, *Latinx Poetics: Essays on the Art of Poetry.* His writing appears in the *New York Times,* Best American Poetry, *American Poetry Review, Kirkus,* and *Harvard Review.* He is a director on the board of the National Book Critics Circle. (*"My Mother Is a Garden,"* 118)

MATT RADER is the author of five collections of poetry, a volume of stories, and a work of nonfiction. He gardens with his family on Syilx territory in present-day Kelowna, British Columbia. (*"Garlic,"* 154)

ANNA V. Q. ROSS'S most recent book, *Flutter, Kick* (Red Hen Press), won the 2020 Benjamin Saltman Poetry Award. Among her honors are fellowships from the Fulbright Foundation and the Massachusetts Cultural Council, and her work appears in *The Nation, Kenyon Review, Southern Review,* and elsewhere. She is poetry editor for *Salamander* and teaches at Tufts University and through the Emerson Prison Initiative. (*"After All,"* 108)

CYNTHIA ROTH was born in Mississippi and grew up in Tennessee. She has won an Illinois Arts Council Individual Artist Fellowship in Poetry and was a Tennessee Williams Scholar in Poetry at the Sewanee Writers' Conference. Her poems have appeared in *Crosswinds, Word Riot, Pittsburgh Quarterly, Moxie,* and other journals. She lives in Murphysboro, Illinois, with her husband and son. (*"In the Dark,"* 76)

JALAL AL-DIN MUHAMMED RUMI (1207–1273) was a Persian poet, Islamic scholar, and Sufi mystic. (from *"You leading the caravan,"* 21)

BRYNN SAITO is the author of *Power Made Us Swoon* (2016) and *The Palace of Contemplating Departure* (2013), winner of the Benjamin Saltman Poetry Award from Red Hen Press and a finalist for the Northern California Book Award. Her third book will be published in late 2023. Brynn is an assistant professor of creative writing at California State University, Fresno. (*"Dear Damselfly,"* 59)

NANAO SAKAKI (1923–2008) was a Japanese poet who traveled a great deal. In the US, he was known partly for his friendship with Allen Ginsburg and Gary Snyder. He spent about 10 years in the US, primarily in San Francisco and Taos, New Mexico, but also walking widely. He was the author of six books of poetry. (*"Just Enough,"* 123)

MARY JO SALTER was born in 1954 in Grand Rapids, Michigan, and grew up there, in Detroit, and in Baltimore. She is the author of nine books of poetry published by Knopf, including *Zoom Rooms* (2022), *The Surveyors* (2017), and *A Phone Call to the Future* (2008). Her book *Nothing by Design* was the recipient of the 2015 Poets' Prize. She is a coeditor of three editions of The Norton Anthology of Poetry and is editor of *Selected Poems of Amy Clampitt*. She retired in 2022 as Krieger-Eisenhower Professor in The Writing Seminars at Johns Hopkins University. (*"Aloe,"* 116)

DEREK SHEFFIELD'S collection *Not for Luck* was selected by Mark Doty for the Wheelbarrow Books Poetry Prize. His other books include *Through the Second Skin*; *Dear America: Letters of Hope, Habitat, Defiance, and Democracy*; and *Cascadia Field Guide: Art, Ecology, Poetry*. The poetry editor of *Terrain .org*, he lives near Leavenworth, Washington, where, much to the delight of the local deer population and with occasional help from his daughters, he keeps a garden. (*"Moon Garden,"* 174)

BRIAN SIMONEAU is the author of the poetry collections *No Small Comfort* (Black Lawrence Press, 2021) and *River Bound* (C&R Press, 2014). His poems have appeared in *Boston Review, Cincinnati Review, Colorado Review, Georgia Review, Salamander, Waxwing,* and other journals. Originally from Lowell, Massachusetts, he lives near Boston with his family. (*"Poem Beginning with a Line from Wordsworth,"* 75)

DEBORAH SLICER is professor emerita at the University of Montana and author of the poetry collection *The White Calf Kicks* (Autumn House Press). (*"Apricot,"* 126)

COLE SWENSEN is the author of 20 volumes, mostly of poetry with inter-mittent essayistic hybridities. Most of her books focus on land, from formal parks (*Greensward, Ours,* and *Park*) to landscape art (*Try, Landscapes on a Train,* and most recently, in 2021, *Art in Time*). A former Guggenheim Fellow and winner of the Iowa Poetry Prize, among other awards, she teaches at Brown University and divides her time between the US and France. (*"Gardening,"* 27)

ARTHUR SZE'S latest book of poetry is *The Glass Constellation: New and Collected Poems* (Copper Canyon Press, 2021). His previous books include *Sight Lines,* which received the 2019 National Book Award for Poetry, *Compass Rose, The Ginkgo Light,* and *Quipu*. A professor emeritus at the Institute of American Indian Arts, he lives in Santa Fe. (*"Oasis,"* 96)

TESS TAYLOR'S five collections of poetry include *The Misremembered World, The Forage House,* and *Work & Days*. In spring 2020, she published two books of poems: *Last West: Roadsongs for Dorothea Lange* (with the

Museum of Modern Art) and *Rift Zone* (named one of the best books of 2020 by *Boston Globe*). Taylor has served as on-air poetry reviewer for NPR's *All Things Considered* for over a decade and is on the faculty of Ashland University's low-residency MFA creative writing program. She gardens and raises chickens in El Cerrito, California, and is helping to restore a community orchard. Follow her at tess-taylor.com and @tessathon. *(Gardening in Public, 13 / "Now the Artichokes," 55 / "Green Tomatoes in Fire Season," 146 / "Turnip Ode," 157)*

ROSEMERRY WAHTOLA TROMMER cohosts the *Emerging Form* podcast on creative process, Secret Agents of Change (a surreptitious kindness cabal), and Soul Writers Circle. Her poetry has appeared on *A Prairie Home Companion, PBS NewsHour, O Magazine, Rattle, American Life in Poetry*, and her daily poetry blog, *A Hundred Falling Veils*. Her most recent collection, *Hush*, won the Halcyon Prize. *Naked for Tea* was a finalist for the Able Muse Book Award. One-word mantra: adjust. *("Three Sunflower Seeds," 28)*

LAURA VILLAREAL is the author of *Girl's Guide to Leaving* (University of Wisconsin Press, 2022). She has received fellowships from the Stadler Center for Poetry & Literary Arts and National Book Critics Circle. Her writing has appeared in *Guernica, American Poetry Review, Waxwing, AGNI*, and elsewhere. *("What Regenerates in a Household," 32)*

VIRGIL (70–19 BCE), whose full name was Publius Vergilius Maro, wrote three of the great classics of Latin literature: the *Aenied*, the *Eclogues*, and the *Georgics*. *("Olives," 197)*

ROSANNA WARREN has published six books of poems, most recently *Ghost in a Red Hat* (2011) and *So Forth* (2020), both from W. W. Norton. *Max Jacob: A Life in Art and Letters*, a biography, was also published by Norton in 2020. *("Season Due," 164)*

CYNTHIA WHITE'S poems have appeared in *Adroit, Massachusetts Review, ZYZZYVA, New Letters*, and *Grist* among others. She was a finalist for both *Nimrod*'s Pablo Neruda Prize and *Slapering Hol*'s 2021 chapbook prize and the winner of the Julia Darling Memorial Prize from Kallisto Gaia Press. She lives in Santa Cruz, California. *("Gardeners' World, or What I Did During the Plague," 101)*

WALT WHITMAN, born on May 31, 1819, is the author of *Leaves of Grass* and, along with Emily Dickinson, is considered one of the architects of a uniquely American poetic voice. (from *"Song of Myself,"* 119)

MAW SHEIN WIN'S most recent poetry book is *Storage Unit for the Spirit House* (Omnidawn), which was nominated for the Northern California Book Award in Poetry, longlisted for the PEN America Open Book Award, and shortlisted for the California Independent Booksellers Alliance's Golden Poppy Award for Poetry. Win's poetry collections also include *Invisible Gifts* and *Score and Bone*. She is the inaugural poet laureate of El Cerrito (2016–2018) and often collaborates with visual artists, musicians, and other writers. See mawsheinwin.com. (*"Thistle,"* 56)

SHOLEH WOLPÉ is an Iranian American poet and playwright. Her most recent book, *Abacus of Loss: A Memoir in Verse* (University of Arkansas Press), is hailed by Ilya Kaminsky as a book "that created its own genre— a thrill of lyric combined with the narrative spell." She is the author or editor of more than a dozen books, several plays, and an opera. Sholeh lives in Los Angeles and Barcelona and is currently a writer-in-residence at University of California, Irvine. (*"The Tulips of Tehran,"* 114)

C. D. WRIGHT (1949–2016), one of the most important poets of her generation, authored more than 20 influential books, including *One With Others* and *One Big Self: Prisoners of Louisiana*. The *New York Times* noted that she "belongs to a school of exactly one." The editor of Lost Roads publishers and a famous teacher at Brown University, she was a social activist and recipient of a Guggenheim Fellowship, a National Book Critics Circle Award, the Griffin Poetry Prize, and a MacArthur Fellowship. (*"Song of the Gourd,"* 72)

GEORGE CEDRIC WRIGHT (1889–1959) was an American violinist, a wilderness photographer, and a dear friend of Ansel Adams. His book *Words of the Earth*, edited by Nancy Newhall, was published by Sierra Club Books in 1960. (from *Words of the Earth*, 1)

JAMES WRIGHT (1927–1980), born in Martins Ferry, Ohio, was a widely admired poet of the postmodern era. His *Collected Poems* won the Pulitzer Prize in poetry in 1972. (Lorca translation, 143)

JENNY XIE is the author of *Eye Level* and *The Rupture Tense*. She lives in New York City. (from *"Tending,"* 46)

Credits

"Pocket Garden in the City," by David Baker, first appeared in *The New Yorker*, and is reprinted by permission of the author.

"Sous-Chef," by Ellen Bass, from *Indigo*. Copyright © 2020 by Ellen Bass. Reprinted with the permission of The Permissions Company, LLC on behalf of Copper Canyon Press, coppercanyonpress.org.

"Ode to the First Peach," by Ellen Bass, from *Like a Beggar*. Copyright © 2014 by Ellen Bass. Reprinted with the permission of The Permissions Company, LLC on behalf of Copper Canyon Press, coppercanyonpress.org.

Excerpt from "Prayers and Sayings of the Mad Farmer," IX, by Wendell Berry, from *New Collected Poems*. Copyright © 1970 by Wendell Berry. Used with the permission of The Permissions Company, LLC on behalf of Counterpoint Press, counterpointpress.com.

"Foreday in the Morning," by Jericho Brown, from *The Tradition*. Copyright © 2019 by Jericho Brown. Reprinted with the permission of The Permissions Company, LLC on behalf of Copper Canyon Press, coppercanyonpress.org. Reproduced with permission of the Licensor through PLSclear.

"Spring Planting," by Victoria Chang, originally appeared in *Ploughshares* (University of Georgia Press).

"cutting greens," by Lucille Clifton, from *How to Carry Water: Selected Poems*. Copyright ©1974, 1987 by Lucille Clifton. Reprinted with the permission

of The Permissions Company, LLC on behalf of BOA Editions, Ltd., boaeditions.org.

"More," by James Crews, from *Bluebird: Poems*, Green Writers Press, 2020.

"Greenbriar Lane," by Diana Marie Delgado, from *Tracing the Horse*. Copyright © 2019 by Diana Marie Delgado. Reprinted with the permission of The Permissions Company, LLC on behalf of BOA Editions, Ltd., boaeditions.org.

"All else is pale echo, dear," by Chiyuma Elliot, originally published in *At Most*, Unicorn Press (2020). Courtesy of Unicorn Press.

"Haecceitas" and "Mississippi Invocation," by Ann Fisher-Wirth, from *The Bones of Winter Birds* (Terrapin Books, 2019). Reprinted by permission of the poet.

Rumi excerpt from "You leading the caravan" from *Gold: Poems from Rumi*, translated by Haleh Liza Gafori. Published by New York Review Books/NYRB Classics. Distributed by Penguin Random House. Copyright © 2022 Haleh Liza Gafori.

Excerpt from "Tell Them No," by Forrest Gander, from *Be With*, New Directions (2018).

"A Small Needful Fact" © 2015 by Ross Gay. First published by Split This Rock. Used by permission of Ross Gay.

"Daffodils," by Michelle Gillett, from *Coming About*. Copyright © 2017 by the Estate of Michelle Gillett. Reprinted with the permission of

Acknowledgments

On the most practical level, I am grateful for hands. This anthology was helped along by Katie Bauer, Conner Davis, Melissa Servey, Simone da Silva, and most particularly Sarah Glanville, to whom I am eternally grateful. I'm also grateful for the use of my neighbor Christine's tiny house, where I had the good fortune to work for some seasons, watching her trees and birds. I'm grateful to the people of the Berkeley Youth Alternatives Community Garden, where I worked twenty years ago and am doing some work now restoring an orchard. I am grateful to Sequence Young for reminding me why gardening together can be a joyful and radical act. I am grateful for my kids, who love worms and chickens, and my partner in life, Taylor, and for all our meals, for the daily act of eating together. Thank you to Hannah Fries and the poets who shared their work and their gifts. Also: I am grateful to soil, microbes, mycorrhizae, groundwater, fog, swallowtail butterflies, the watershed, the bee, the sage, the tomato. May we steward all these. May we feed one another well. May the good ecosystem hold.

VIRGIL

Olives

—*Georgics, 2.420–25*

Olives, by contrast, need no care,
don't call for machete or stubborn hoe—
once they've clung to the fields & bowed with the breezes
the Earth, which the plowshare exposed,
of herself offers up moist, heavy fruit.

O, suckle the olive: fat, pleasing to Peace.

The mission of Storey Publishing is to serve our customers by publishing practical information that encourages personal independence in harmony with the environment.

Edited by Hannah Fries

Art direction and book design by Carolyn Eckert

Production design by Jennifer Jepson Smith

Illustrations by © Melissa Castrillón 2023

Text © 2023 *by* Tess Taylor

Storey books are available at special discounts when purchased in bulk for premiums and sales promotions as well as for fund-raising or educational use. Special editions or book excerpts can also be created to specification. For details, please send an email to special.markets@hbgusa.com.

STOREY PUBLISHING
210 MASS MoCA Way
North Adams, MA 01247
storey.com

Storey Publishing, LLC is an imprint of Workman Publishing Co., Inc., a subsidiary of Hachette Book Group, Inc., 1290 Avenue of the Americas, New York, NY 10104

ISBNs: 978-1-63586-580-6 (hardcover with ribbon bookmark); 978-1-63586-581-3 (ebook)

Printed in China by R. R. Donnelley

10 9 8 7 6 5 4 3 2 1

Library of Congress Cataloging-in-Publication Data on file

Tess Taylor, an avid gardener, is also the author of
five acclaimed collections of poetry.
Taylor is currently on the faculty of Ashland University's
low-residency MFA in Creative Writing program.
She grew up and lives again in El Cerrito, California, where she tends
to several fruit trees and four backyard chickens.

Illustrated by Melissa Castrillón,
an English and Colombian illustrator based in the southeast of England,
who spends her days illustrating and
writing books that are published all around the world.

This book is set in Arno Pro, an old-style serif font, designed by
Robert Slimbach, who was inspired by the typefaces of the
fifteenth and sixteenth centuries. Its name comes from the river that runs
through Florence, a center of the Italian Renaissance.

JOHN KEATS

On the Grasshopper and Cricket

The Poetry of earth is never dead:
  When all the birds are faint with the hot sun,
  And hide in cooling trees, a voice will run
From hedge to hedge about the new-mown mead;
That is the Grasshopper's—he takes the lead
  In summer luxury,—he has never done
  With his delights; for when tired out with fun
He rests at ease beneath some pleasant weed.
The poetry of earth is ceasing never:
  On a lone winter evening, when the frost
    Has wrought a silence, from the stove there shrills
The Cricket's song, in warmth increasing ever,
  And seems to one in drowsiness half lost,
    The Grasshopper's among some grassy hills.